DIANE RUDOLPH

SUCCEED IN THE BUSINESS WORLD

DISCOVER YOUR
PROFESSIONAL CALLING

Succeed in the Business World – *Discover Your Professional Calling*

Copyright ©2020 by Beautiful Works Publishing

Published by Beautiful Works Publishing, Farmington Hills, MI

All rights reserved. No part of this publication may be reproduced, distributed, or transmitted in any form or by any means, including photocopying, recording, or other electronic or mechanical methods, without the prior written permission of the author, except in the case of brief quotations embodied in critical reviews and certain other noncommercial uses permitted by copyright law.

For information, contact Beautiful Works Publishing – dara@beautifulworkspublishing.com.

The advice, information and opinions offered by Diane Rudolph are intended to be general information and does not constitute legal or professional advice, neither is it intended to be. Advice, information and opinions are offered in good faith and you do not have to follow such. You have your own free will. Any decisions you make, and the consequences thereof are your own. Under no circumstances can you hold Diane Rudolph liable for any action that you take. You agree not to hold Diane Rudolph liable for any lost or any cost incurred by you, or any person related or associated with you, as a result of materials or techniques offered by Diane Rudolph.

Formatting: Ya Ya Ya Creative – www.yayayacreative.com

ISBN No. 978-0-578-62605-5

PRINTED AND BOUND IN THE UNITED STATES OF AMERICA

ACKNOWLEDGEMENTS

I'm so very grateful to the Lord for giving me the inspiration to author this book. His loving hand guided me through the entire process. This book is a tribute to the Lord and a stepping stone to what He has in store for me. I thank my Pastor, Dr. Gertrude Stacks, for the instructions the Lord gave her for me. Those instructions set this book in motion and brought it to full fruition. To my husband, Elder Dennis Rudolph, your love and support have been absolutely amazing. Your prayers have been my strength. I'm so grateful that I have a praying man by my side. My late mother, Janet Irene Williams, encouraged me immensely to follow my dreams. I thank God for the writing gift that my mother possessed and passed down to me. To my sisters, Deborah and Margo, thanks for keeping me on course. Your pep talks, prayers, and support were greatly appreciated. My loving children, Dennis, Jennifer, and Kristina, thank you for sharing me with the work the

Lord has given me to do. I appreciate the contribution that each of you made to my book. I will forever be grateful to my family, friends, and my wonderful church family, who has always loved and supported me.

INTRODUCTION

I was inspired to write this book so I could share my experiences with others who are looking for more career options and want to enhance their professional skills. Career and professional development have always been my passion. I use every opportunity to inspire, motivate, and encourage individuals who are searching for the career of their dreams or assistance with their current careers. It doesn't matter if you're sweeping a floor or answering phones in an office, you can find your professional calling and have a fulfilling career. This book will assist you with that process. Everyone's journey on their career path is unique and personal. I hope my journey encourages, empowers, and energizes you.

My journey to my professional calling is the foundation of this book. I will cover how I embarked on my career, my experiences, and how to find your professional calling. I will also discuss the principles of business character and how they are essential to your growth and professional development. I have included several career testimonies from successful colleagues and friends who have experienced the same frustrations you and I may have experienced during our careers. These individuals were resilient and are now enjoying successful careers. And I will share much more.

This is a faith-based book. I encourage my readers to achieve their dreams through faith and belief in themselves and the abilities they possess. The business principles are universal, and everyone, from all walks of life, can gleam and prosper by applying them.

The effective tools you will gain from this book will not only launch you into your professional calling, but they will empower you to *Succeed in the Business World*. Your professional calling is your passion and your dream career. My professional calling was a career in human resources. It's time for you to discover yours.

This is your opportunity to change your career path and your life. You can be successful.

Let's get started!

TABLE OF CONTENTS

Acknowledgements iii

Introduction v

Chapter 1—Are You Ready For a Career Change? 1

Chapter 2—Discover Your Professional Calling 15

Chapter 3—Welcome to The Business World 29

Chapter 4—The Principles of Business Character 43

Chapter 5—Professional Business Image 71

Chapter 6—Master Your Soft Skills 87

Chapter 7—Your Gift Will Make Room For You 99

Chapter 8—Success Is Waiting On You 131

Chapter 9—The Secrets of Your Professional Calling 139

Chapter 10—The Takeaway 149

CHAPTER 1
ARE YOU READY FOR A CAREER CHANGE?

A career is a speed in a course, a passage, encounter, and charge. The progression of your career is your **speed**, how swiftly you move from one position to another. Your speed is based on several elements: your impetus to excel and your drive for success. Your **course** defines the class you're in. To be successful, you must pass every class. In college, you take classes and receive either a passing or failing grade. You can't move ahead if you're failing classes. When you've passed every class of a position, you're ready for the next. Usually, you can't be promoted until you've demonstrated mastery in your current position. **Passage** is the action or process of passing from one place, condition, or stage to another. That's exactly what you want to do, move from one stage or position to another. Sometimes you may move from one location to another or one position to another and maintain the same salary. Those are opportunities as well because of the learning curve that comes with each move. To **encounter** means to meet an adversary or enemy. During your career, you will contend with many adversaries such as problematic situations, challenges, and difficult tests, not to mention the colleagues who just don't like you. It's impossible for everyone to like you, but it's not impossible for everyone to respect you. I would rather have respect. Likes and dislikes are here today and gone tomorrow. However, true respect builds bridges. Finally, **charge** means the responsibility of managing or watching over something. Your career and what you do with it is your responsibility. You are in control of managing and taking charge of your career. What you invest is what you'll get back. The right investments last a lifetime.

Trapped in a Barrel

I was working as a senior-level office assistant at a government agency, and I was at the top of my position. I loved my job. My office, coworkers, and manager were great. As an office assistant, I dressed and conducted myself like a professional. I had a small staff under me, and I was familiar with organizing and delegating. I was always eager to take on extra projects, and I was the head of the office for approximately thirty-five engineers and drafting technicians. Even though I was a senior office assistant, I worked in the capacity of an office manager. I acted as a liaison between the engineering staff and human resources, handling all the HR issues such as vacation time, sick time, promotions, and retirement.

My manager gave me quite a bit of flexibility, but I had outgrown the position. I wanted to learn and do new things, and there was nothing else for me in that position. I felt trapped. I managed the division office and clerical unit, which included the engineering office and print room. I was also involved in several special projects, and I was the department representative at many of my company's fundraisers and events. Through my efforts, the department received many awards for special achievements during the company's campaign charity drives.

I was not the typical office assistant. The duties I took on were above that. I could feel a shift in my spirit. It wasn't enough anymore. I needed more challenges from my career. I could perform all my duties with my eyes closed, and I had achieved everything I could as a clerical employee. My coworkers seemed content where they were. We all talked about going back to school and having professional careers, but no one made any initiatives toward those goals.

I had a few opportunities to move up, but something always blocked me from being promoted. We had gotten a new manager, and he was so impressed with my efficiency in the office that he recommended me for a promotion. My other managers were accustomed to my high level of performance, but this manager wanted to do something about it. He requested that my job be surveyed by the human resources department to promote me to a higher position.

The process was going great until one of the other clerical employees in my division went to the manager and requested a survey for her position as well. I asked her to wait until my survey was done because two upgrades in the same budget year were difficult to achieve. She didn't want to wait, and she felt if I was being considered for a promotion, so should she. Both of our positions were surveyed together. After the survey analysis was complete, HR recommended me for a promotion and my coworker for a demotion, or the manager could leave us in our same positions. What a mess! Of course, my manager chose the latter because, as he informed me, my coworker was a single mother and couldn't afford a demotion. I was so disappointed. Why didn't she listen to me?

In another situation when I was being considered for a promotion, I had passed the exam and interview process to become a claims investigator. It wasn't a professional position; however, it was technical, and it would take me out of the clerical group and to a new division. Normally, professional positions required a four-year degree, technical positions required a certification or a two-year degree, and clerical required no degree at all but training and experience. Our department was small, and everyone knew each other. One of the candidates had already worked in the position I had applied for, but she hadn't passed her probationary period, and she lost the job. I found out during the interview process that she was allowed to work in the position even though the department had deemed her unqualified. While working in the position, she received the pay for the position as well, which is known as working out-of-class. Demoting her but allowing her to work out-of-class was like saying she wasn't capable of performing the job permanently, but she could work in the position temporarily. It didn't make sense. Either you're qualified or you're not. This didn't sit well with me.

We both applied for the position, and after the interviews were complete, I was offered the job. I had to think about it because I felt the department was using me to block the other candidate from getting her position back. I wanted a promotion badly, so it was a hard decision to make. It seemed I kept getting cheated out of my opportunities. When I had been up for promotion previously, my coworker didn't do the right thing. But even though she hadn't done the right thing before, I had to do the right thing now. I had to stop the vicious cycle.

It reminded me of the metaphor "crabs in a barrel." All the crabs were trying to climb out of the barrel, but none of them could get out because they were pulling each other down. This was my opportunity to help someone else climb out of the barrel. The young woman had been unfairly treated and used by the department, and I was not going to pull her back down, so I declined the promotion. The director's facial expression told me I would never get another offer there. Regardless, I still had to do the right thing. The director offered the other young lady the position, and she accepted it. She thanked me for not taking the position because she felt she wasn't given a fair chance during her first probationary period. The supervisor who had demoted her had retired, and there was a new supervisor in her place. This time, she passed her probation with flying colors, and she went on to become the supervisor of the entire unit. We are still friends to this day.

My Breaking Point

Yes, I had done the right thing, but I was still stuck in my current position and going nowhere fast. I called the pension office and inquired about my retirement benefits. The clerk informed me that with my current salary, my retirement income would be about $14,000 a year. I was shocked.

"Are you sure?" I asked.

I'll never forget her response. "You're only in a clerical position."

When I got off the phone, I said to myself, "Only a clerical position ... Not for long."

I realized I could no longer sit around and wait for opportunities to come my way. I had to make things happen for myself by changing my situation. I declared, that day, that I was going back to school. I had already earned an associate's degree in business management at Wayne County Community College. I decided to get a bachelor's degree. It was my *only* way out of the barrel. I was ready for change and determined to get a professional position. I prayed and asked God about my education and the path I should take. The answer became clear, and I felt led to pursue my education. I was happy because I knew the Lord had answered my prayers.

I was thirty-eight years old. I had a husband, three children under the age of twelve, and a full-time job. I couldn't consider a regular university. On the radio, I had heard about accelerated bachelor's degree programs. To qualify, a certain amount of college credits were required. I had an associate's degree, which qualified me. I searched for accelerated degree programs, and for the first few colleges I contacted, their business programs weren't in business administration but other related studies. I wanted a degree in business administration because it encompassed everything from accounting, marketing, finances, human resources, planning and development, and so on. Plus, it was a well-recognized degree in the business industry.

Finally, I contacted William Tyndale College in Farmington Hills, MI. The college offered an accelerated degree program for business administration. It was eighteen months long with several modules to be completed within that time. It sounded great, so I enrolled.

The curriculum entailed a lot of reading and writing. The class met four hours a week, every Wednesday evening from six p.m. to ten p.m. My husband worked afternoons, so he wasn't available to keep the children. The modules were held in the Farmington Hills area, and my sister's house was just fifteen minutes away, depending on traffic. I talked to my sister and her husband, and they were more than willing to assist me. On Wednesdays after work, I picked the kids up from latchkey and drove straight to my sister's house. When I arrived, dinner was always prepared for the children and me. I drove to the school after dinner, and after class, I picked up the kids and headed back home. The kids and I would get home at close to eleven p.m. Wednesdays were long days, but the sacrifice was worth it.

I kept up the routine for eighteen months, only missing one class during the entire program because I was sick at the ER. I didn't play around when it came to my education. Finally, all my hard work paid off. I earned my bachelor's degree in business administration. I graduated cum laude right before I turned forty years old. What an accomplishment! I was so proud. I was getting closer to my goal.

Climbing Out

Now that I had my bachelor's degree, I wanted to be promoted to a professional position within my company. Many said it would be impossible because everyone was accustomed to seeing me as a clerical employee. Others said very few employees had made the transition from clerical to professional. It was more common to be promoted from a clerical position to technical then to a professional position. That was the acceptable hierarchy of promotion in my company—step by step, no jumping. I didn't have time for that. I was determined to go from clerical to professional no matter what it took.

I applied for professional positions for two years without any success until I saw a job posting that would change my life: HR consultant for the human resources department. After reading the job specifications, I thought, *Wow! I would love this position.* The HR consultant position was all about people and providing them with quality service. Whether it was recruitment, promotions, benefits, or career development, the HR consultant assisted employees with the tools they needed to be successful in their careers and personal lives. The position was everything I wanted. The educational requirement was a bachelor's degree, and I now met the qualification. The experience requirement wasn't going to be a problem because I had been an HR liaison for my division for years. Several departments needed HR consultants, and when I applied, I didn't select a preference for any department. I didn't care where I was assigned; I just felt the position was for me. On the application, I listed all the qualifying experience I'd acquired while working for the engineering division. I had assisted employees with payroll issues, applications for retirement, wage and promotion adjustments, sick and vacation time issues, and more. My department was the only one where the payroll entry had to be entered in another system and performed by clerical staff, not the payroll staff in HR. I handled the payroll entry weekly, and it gave me an edge in HR experience.

My coworker who had gotten the position as the investigator was good friends with an administrator, and she sent several recommendations to the administrator on my behalf—another push out of the barrel. You reap what you sow. I had helped her out of the barrel, and now she was helping me.

The human resources department contacted me and gave me an interview date and time. Going into the interview, I was nervous. There were three people on the interview panel from various departments, two men and one woman.

They asked several questions, and I answered them all well. Of course, the panel asked about my HR experience. I had never worked in HR; however, I magnified any experience I had that mirrored HR functions. I reiterated to the panel what I had stated on my application, that I was the HR liaison for the engineering division and what that entailed. I also stated that I imputed the payroll for my department on a weekly basis. I didn't have any problems with their questions. I was calm, confident, and articulate. One question did throw me because they asked me the meaning of a term I didn't know. I analyzed the sentence and gave the answer based on context clues. I could tell by their faces I had answered correctly.

When I left the interview, I felt like I was high in the sky, like I could accomplish anything. With a sense of newness and confidence, I knew my change was on the way.

Standing on the Edge

I waited patiently for the results of my interview. About six weeks later, I received a letter that stated I had successfully passed the interview process. I could feel it; I was on my way to becoming a professional business woman. I couldn't wait.

The next step was a written exam, but that obstacle was not a problem. I was ready for anything. To prepare for the exam, I studied the HR rules, policies, and practices. I didn't feel comfortable asking the HR consultant assigned to my department because she would've probably questioned my motive for the information. I wanted to keep everything confidential. I had a friend downtown who worked in HR, and she gave me the HR rules and practices manual. I studied the manual for weeks. On the day of the test, I arrived at 8:30 a.m. There were twelve of us taking the exam. I assumed all the other candidates had been interviewed and were successful as well.

The first portion of the exam was multiple choice, and each section was timed. I did well, answering all the questions within the given timeframe. The next phase of the exam was an essay. I hated writing, but I was prepared. We were required to write an essay on an HR function or practice. My head was full of HR practices I had studied. We were given lined paper and pencils to write by hand, which was difficult because I was a typist. I wrote until I had hand cramps. When I finally finished, it was 12:30 p.m., and I was exhausted, but I knew I had done a good job.

Taking that Leap

I felt anxious, excited, and optimistic for the next few weeks while I waited for my results. Finally, the HR consultant in my department called me and asked me to come to her office. Going to the HR consultant's office was always a big deal because she handled all the HR processes for the entire department. When we were called to her office, it was usually for something bad or good. When I arrived, she showed me the paperwork that stated I was being promoted to an HR consultant.

It felt surreal! The Lord had blessed me, and I finally had a professional position within my company. It was amazing because I had gone from clerical to professional instead of the usual path. I didn't pull anyone down to get the position. I'd earned it from working hard and going after my dream. I was told that I was the only one promoted out of that group of twelve with whom I'd taken the exam. I was stunned!

Before I signed the document, the HR representative asked, "Are you sure you know what you're doing?"

I looked her directly in her eyes. "Yes, I do."

I proceeded to sign. Why wouldn't I be good enough to have the same position she had. Everyone wanted to keep me in a box, in my own little world. I had been in the same department for many years; I was ready and eager to leave, to meet new people and learn new things. I was ready to take a leap into a new profession and career, and it felt so good! I knew this new position was going to come with challenges, and that was probably what she'd meant, but I was ready for the challenge. This was my new beginning.

Many of my coworkers were happy for me. It was a joyous time. I was finally out of the barrel!

My department gave me a huge going away party, and everyone was there. I felt so much love. I thought, *Oh, my God! Success feels great!* This was the beginning of my professional calling.

CHAPTER 2
DISCOVER YOUR PROFESSIONAL CALLING

Finding a career path that makes us feel satisfied and successful isn't easy. It's not something they teach us in school, which makes the journey that much more challenging. We spend one-third (or more) of our days at work. Work defines us as people, i.e. when we aren't happy at work, other areas of our life suffer. Yet more than seventy percent of workers say they don't feel satisfied with their career choices, and I believe we have a serious epidemic on our hands.

–O'DONNELL, 2018

What's a Calling?

Many people associate a calling with a religious call to ministry. I agree with that, but a call has a natural and spiritual purpose. We must fulfill both; however, the Bible says first natural then spiritual. Here, we will address the natural calling and purpose, which concentrates on your profession and career. A calling is a strong desire to spend your life doing a certain kind of work such as becoming a teacher, lawyer, author, businessman or woman, or doing skilled trades. Your hands may be gifted for culinary arts, designing, engineering, fine arts, and so much more. Many entrepreneurs have found their callings in the businesses they've started in fields such as IT services, event planning, day care, restaurants, or website developer.

I always knew I wanted to rise to the level of a business professional. When I was in college, I wrote my thesis on that very subject. The desire was in my heart back then, but I had to make it happen. Many of us know deep down that we're meant to do more with our careers and professions than what we're doing.

I was in a class that my pastor, Dr. Gertrude Stacks, was teaching. She asked the class to write the first word that came into our minds. I wrote "industrious," which means working very hard, not lazy, being skillful and diligent. I was an office assistant at the time, but I was destined to do more with my life. When you desire something, it's a part of you. That's why that word was inside of me. My industrious qualities were destined to lead me to my professional calling.

Why Do You Need to Be Industrious?

Simply put, a lazy person will never discover their professional calling. They're too lazy to put in the hard work, energy, and time it takes to research, meditate, pray, and study to find out what they're destined to do with their life. You might say you're not lazy and you work hard every day to provide for you and your family, and that may be true, but think about it: Are you complacent? Do you talk about wanting opportunities to do more with your life but fail to go after those opportunities? Are you trapped in a job you don't want to be in? That's exactly how I felt until I decided to do something about it. Don't be complacent and just accept the status quo. An industrious individual is not lazy or complacent, but diligent. This is not a game. This is your life and future. You must be dedicated and willing to sacrifice to make things happen for yourself. You must be consistent and steadfast in your endeavors to achieve what's best for you.

You may be thinking, *How can I change?* You can learn good habits; therefore, you can learn to be industrious. You must be focused to get to your professional calling.

TIPS FOR BEING INDUSTRIOUS:

- ✓ Energize yourself about the things that are important to you
- ✓ Be diligent about your goals and dreams
- ✓ Put your time in, and do your homework
- ✓ Be disciplined, and stay on track
- ✓ Stay devoted to a task until it's complete

Your Professional Calling

Now that you've learned the *qualities* of being industrious, you're ready to discover your professional calling. Right now, you may not have a clue about what your calling is, but it is right in front of you in some way, shape, or form. When I completed my degree, I wasn't sure which way I was going. All I knew was I wanted to advance in my company on a professional level. I didn't know what position, area, or expertise I would need. Where you are now will help you get to where you're going. Even if you hate the job you have now, you have acquired some skillsets along the way that will assist you in your new job or business. No experience or training is wasted time. It's all beneficial in the long run.

I once listened to a commencement speech from Steve Jobs, and he said, "You can't connect the dots looking forward, only looking back." This is true regarding your career because the experience and skillsets you are acquiring now will connect to your future. All the dots will eventually connect for you.

TOOLS TO HELP YOU DISCOVER YOUR PROFESSIONAL CALLING:

1. **Assess your situation.**
   Do a total assessment of your current job and company. Ask yourself these questions: Do you love your job? Do you have more likes than dislikes or the inverse regarding your employer? Does your current position give you a sense of purpose? Are the salary and benefits meeting all your needs? Are there opportunities for growth and advancement in your company? If your answers are mostly yes, you may choose to make plans to stay at your current company and pursue other opportunities or areas of interest right there. If most of your answers are no, you should prepare to explore other options outside of the company. Be open minded.

2. **Think about what inspires you.**
   Ask yourself what you like doing or what inspires you. Do you love working with people, or do you prefer to work alone? Start thinking about what you're passionate about. I'm sure there is a career out there that fits your interests.

3. **Look at your strengths.**

   Ask yourself what you're good at. What gets your juices flowing? Are you a good planner, organizer, or writer? Do you like working with your hands? Do you have an analytical mind? Take a good look at all your strengths, and write each one down. You can match them up with careers that best suit you.

4. **Get career counseling.**

   Career counseling can help you identify the best profession for you. The counselor will take a complete inventory of your personality and abilities. The career counselor may also recommend taking a career test and make career suggestions based on the results of the assessment. Some agencies charge a fee, but free career counseling is also available.

5. **Consider more training or education.**

   Be open to additional training or education. This depends on the career you're considering. Training and education are good investments, but make sure you've made a solid decision regarding your career choice before committing to going back to school. Some employers offer tuition reimbursement, or your employer may offer training for employees who want to enhance their skillsets. Take full advantage of the perks your current employer offers. Most importantly, do your research on the career of your choice, and make sure there are plenty of jobs available in the market before you invest in the training or education.

6. **Explore entrepreneurship.**
   Consider starting your own business. Do you want to be your own boss and shape your own career? What services or products would you offer? The small business market is booming, but you have to find a solid niche. Some colleges offer entrepreneurship classes and certifications. Be in the know about the legal, marketing, and investment strategies required to launch a successful business. Learn all the aspects of starting your own business. Often, the best way to start your business is on the weekends while you're still fully employed. That way, you'll still have your bread-and-butter job while trying out your new business venture. See how the business progresses and decide whether you want to pursue it full-time.

7. **Listen to your heart.**
   Remember to listen to your heart. Spend some time with yourself. Quiet your mind and think about you. What is your heart saying, and what is your desire? Stop listening to logic, and listen to your heart. Your passion flows from your heart. Don't take on a career that your heart isn't into because you won't give it your all. It's

good to listen to the opinions of others, but at the end of the day, you've got to follow your heart. Steve Jobs once said, "Don't let the noise of others' opinions drown out your own inner voice. And most importantly, have the courage to follow your heart and intuition."

8. **Ask the Lord for guidance.**
    Last but not least, pray! Ask the Lord to guide you. "Ask, and it shall be given you; seek, and ye shall find; knock, and it shall be opened unto you" (Matthew 7:7 KJV). Acknowledge Him and tell Him about your career dreams.

I encourage you to weigh and explore all your options. You may discover your professional calling at any time, whether early on or later in life. There is no time limit. However, that doesn't give you an excuse to procrastinate. Time is valuable. The sooner you get down to business, the better, especially when there's a desire burning inside you. I didn't make a career change until I was thirty-eight, and that's considered late, but it was the right time for me, and it yielded some of the best years of my life.

Making the Decision

The first step is knowing what you want to do with your career, knowing what your professional calling is. It's a big decision. When you decide on your career, it will ultimately change your life. It's not an easy decision. Don't rush! You must think and take your time. Be patient, do your research, pray, and search your heart. When you make the final decision, it should bring you peace of mind or a sense of relief because you are on your way.

The decision should also bring you joy. When I decided to go back to school and complete my business degree, I was ecstatic. I told all my family and friends because I could see the light at the end of the tunnel. I was so excited that I even told my manager. I wanted everyone to know. But when I saw the expression on his face, I knew that telling him wasn't such a good idea. Your decision should energize you and make you happy. If it doesn't, you will need to go back and start again.

You must be determined to not remain in your situation or your present job forever. It's time to get energized now because you have plans to make and places to go.

Having a Plan

When you select your professional calling, you must lay out a strategy to get there. In other words, you must plan and take action. For example, if you've selected a career that requires you to go back to school, you should start searching for a college or university that can accommodate your needs. If you're currently working, you may want to consider online or evening courses. If you're starting a business, learn how to create a business plan. There's a ton of information online from organizations that will assist you with the process. Reach out to successful entrepreneurs and ask for advice about starting your business. If you're applying for new career opportunities, be prepared for the interview process and revamp your résumé.

Your plan to reach your professional calling should consist of the following:

1. **Setting Goals**

    Set SMART goals. According to mindtools.com, SMART is the acronym for S – Specific, M – Measurable, A - Attainable, and R – Relevant, and T - Time-Bound (SMART Goals, 2019).

    a. **Specific**

    Your goal should be specific. You must know exactly what you want to achieve. Goals too broad in range may cause you to lose focus. The goals should be concrete and clear, helping you to stay motivated and on task. While preparing your goals, remember the five "W" questions:

    - What do I want to achieve?
    - Why is this goal significant to me?
    - Who is playing a part in this?

- Where will this take me?
- Which resources are needed to accomplish my goal?

b. **Measurable**

Set goals that are measurable, and think about how you're going to gauge yourself to achieve your goals. Consider the degree of time, money, and energy required to accomplish your goals. Then measure all those things against your lifestyle and income. By assessing your goals, you'll know exactly what your limits and boundaries are.

c. **Achievable**

Is your goal realistic? Don't set a goal that is impossible to achieve. An achievable goal sets you up for success and puts things into prospective because you'll know you have the ability and resources to accomplish your desired outcome.

d. **Relevant**

Pursue meaningful goals. You want to ensure that the goal is worth your time and effort. Aim for goals that have purpose in your life and align with your career path. Also, it's important to consider whether your endeavors are applicable to the current business industry.

e. **Time-Bound**

   Timing is important. Don't put your goals on hold for too long. Set a start and completion date. A time-bound goal may be completed in six months or six weeks depending on the task. Lengthy time-bound goals may take twelve to twenty-four months. It depends on what you're striving to accomplish. If you don't have time parameters, you can't control the outcome. Most importantly, start thinking about what you can do today to set things in motion.

Now that you know how to set SMART goals, let's move forward to the next phase of our plan.

2. **Taking Action**

   Write your goals in a journal, hardcopy or electronic. Some people like using Post-It notes to write their goals and thoughts. Do what works for you. Writing it makes it real and tangible. Take your time and write out a step-by-step action plan to reaching your goal. I love writing in my journal. When I need a boost, I can always go back to my journal for reflection and inspiration. I can also see what I've already accomplished. Share your journal with someone you trust like a mentor or close friend to seal the deal. When you speak your dreams verbally, you put those words into the atmosphere.

3. **Following Through**

    After you have established your goal, stay committed to the plan you've put into place. This is the most challenging phase of accomplishing your goals because life can throw so many obstacles in your way. Your dream should always be in the forefront of your mind, no matter what happens. Following through, for me, was doing the research to find a college program that met my needs and taking the step to enroll despite the challenges I faced with my family's schedule. You must stay focused and follow through on your plans every step of the way. Review your plans regularly to help you stay on track.

4. **Getting Results**

    Each time you accomplish a step in your plan, you're getting results. Celebrate each step by rewarding yourself because you deserve it. All the big and small results are leading to a great outcome. My small results were passing each module in my course plan, and my big result was the day I graduated with a bachelor's degree in business administration.

KEY POINTS

- *What's a calling?*—Do you know what your calling is?

- *Industrious*—Understanding what it takes to get to your calling.
- *Discovering your professional calling*—Having the necessary tools to guide you.
- *Deciding*—Knowing what's right for you.
- *Having a plan*—Setting into place the parameters that will take you to a positive outcome.

CHAPTER 3
WELCOME TO THE BUSINESS WORLD

The Transition

It may be a new position, new profession, or a new business, but when it happens, you're going to find yourself in a whole new world. You've found something that didn't exist in your life before. It's like wearing a new pair of shoes. Sometimes new shoes hurt but you love them, and you'll keep wearing them until they're perfectly comfortable. Newness brings transition. I want you to be prepared for it. The transition from your old job to your new career or business is going to rock your world. You didn't take a small step or jump; you took a leap. When you leap into something, you defy the laws of gravity. I'll share my career transition experience to assist you with yours.

I was promoted from an office assistant to a human resources consultant. The specifications for the two positions were drastically different. As an office assistant, I managed the clerical functions of my assigned division. As a human resources consultant, I reported directly to the department heads and was responsible for their staffing budgets, recruitment strategies, disciplinary actions, grievances, employee trainings, and contract negotiations. At first, it was difficult to see my way because I was in uncharted waters. My work attire changed also. In my former position, I wore suits a few times a month. Now, I wore them every day. My schedule was driven by deadlines and weekly and monthly reports. I received calls all day from department and division heads regarding issues and employee situations that needed my attention. Employees called daily to make appointments and discuss personal HR issues. Some employees showed up at the office without appointments. We called them walk-ins. No one was turned away. I had so many assignments and tasks to complete that my head was spinning. I wasn't accustomed to a fast-paced work day. It was a 180-degree turnaround.

My former job was easy. I had everything wrapped around my pinkie finger, and I performed the job exceptionally, so I had leisure time because I knew my job so well. On my two fifteen-minute breaks, which I rarely missed, I would take naps for a total of thirty minutes of nap time at work, and I always took my one-hour lunch break. Things were different now.

I had a difficult schedule, but I battled through each day. I had to break the old mold to which I was accustomed. No naps! I soon realized I was spoiled in my former position, but I was focused on breaking that mold. With each day I conquered, I felt a renewed sense of energy for the next. I was determined to master and tame this new career. I had to get through the transition, no matter how daunting, because it was my new career, and I loved it! This was what I wanted and what I had been waiting for. I wasn't going to let anything stop me, not even me.

The Battle

Getting where you want to go in life or your career isn't easy. You have to fight for what you want. Some days, you're going to feel like giving up. You're going to think it's too hard. Sometimes, I felt like that. I'd think, *I can't keep up with all of this.* However, I never let the thoughts over take me. I always persevered and said, "I can do this." You've got to talk to yourself and say you can do it. Each time you speak to yourself with encouragement, you're gaining ground. You're winning the battle. When you're chasing a dream—perhaps getting married, having a baby, buying a new home, or starting a new career—you must make a sacrifice for the dream. New responsibilities come with achieving dreams. You must work hard to get your blessing and keep the blessing. To make it work, you've got to give it your all. That's the only way you're going to succeed with life's blessings. Many entrepreneurs put in a ton of hours each week to achieve success in their business, and they love it. It's their dream, their calling, and they're not going to give up.

Another battle was my six-month probationary period, a trial period to test my skills and abilities to do the job. My supervisor filled out documents to evaluate my performance during the six-month period. At the end of that period, my supervisor would recommend one of three choices for my employment: 1.) Become permanent in the position; 2.) Extend the probationary period due to work performance or other issues (must be documented); 3.) Be reverted to the previous position, which meant failing the probationary period. I was nervous and wanted to get everything right. About four months into my probation, my colleague came into my office and said, "You know you're allowed to take a vacation day." Everyone was taking time off but me, but I felt that while on probation, it was my opportunity to prove to my colleagues and managers that I was worthy of the position. I didn't want to miss anything. Attendance and dedication to the job is critical to your success in any position. My colleagues pressed me to give myself a rest. I did eventually take a few days of vacation, but I remained dedicated and committed to my new career.

The Learning Curve

There was so much to learn! The HR department had numerous processes, and they were constantly updating. I worked for a contract-driven agency. Most of the employees were under a contract or a CBA (collective bargaining agreement). There were approximately thirty or more CBA departments agency-wide, which didn't include the supplemental agreements (small contracts for a particular department). Also, there were twenty-five or more HR processes and rules along with agency-wide rules and executive orders. My training was intense. I always took notes because it was easy to forget what someone had rattled off to me in a five-minute meeting. My manager was an excellent teacher, but she didn't have a lot of time to spend with me. Her schedule was hectic. Whatever I learned from her, I had to learn quickly. I always took a pen and pad into her office so I could take notes. I made lists of all the questions I had prior to meeting with her, so I wouldn't forget anything while I was in her office. Everyone's time is precious, and I may have had only one opportunity to speak with her that day. I kept detailed notes and studied the manuals, contracts, and processes.

I didn't know it all; I had to learn. I relied on my support staff's assistance for certain issues. Our clerical and payroll teams were good sources of information, and they were knowledgeable about the processes. I also relied on my colleagues who had more experience and were willing to share that experience. Always use the resources available to you.

Mistakes

Even while being careful and diligent, you will make mistakes because you're new to the arena. I made a mistake during an internal recruitment for summer technicians that was only open to the department. The recruitment was successful. We had six open positions, and over fifty applicants applied. Approximately fourteen out of the fifty were cleared as qualified applicants. After the interview process was complete, I made a spreadsheet with all the applicants and their interview scores. It was a manual process, not a computerized program. I wanted to fit all the information on a single-paged spreadsheet. I decided to use the candidates' first initial and last name. I didn't realize that two of the candidates had the same first initial and last name. I had put too much effort into the aesthetic appeal of the spreadsheet and not enough into the accuracy. I prepared a beautiful spreadsheet to present to the director and my manager with all the candidates' scores. At the meeting, my manager began discussing the recruitment, and a particular candidate came into question.

Chapter 3—WELCOME TO THE BUSINESS WORLD

My manager looked at me and said, "His score doesn't look right. I thought he had scored higher. Please go to your office and check the original documents."

When I got to my office and looked at the documents, I realized I had transposed the candidate in question's score with another candidate with the same first initial and last name. I could've screamed. I thought, *Oh, my God! I have to go back in that meeting and tell everyone what happened.* I swallowed the big lump of pride in my throat and returned to the meeting with the documents, and I immediately told everyone what happened. The director didn't look at me; he just looked down.

I felt like sliding under the table and hiding there until the meeting was over. This was my first recruitment, and I had blown it. It was a mistake, and mistakes happen, but no one came to me and said, "Oh, this was your first recruitment; it's okay." There were no encouraging words. Don't expect it from anyone else; do it yourself. Encourage yourself. Be your number one cheerleader! You've got to face your mistakes and learn from them. But most importantly, get over it. Don't let it hold you down. I managed countless successful recruitments afterwards without any errors.

The Strategy

To complete all my assignments on their targeted dates, I developed a strategy, which consisted of organization, time management, delegation, limitations, and networking.

STEP ONE: *Organization*

I had to organize all the tools I needed for my job, or I was going to be lost. I was servicing three or four small departments, with approximately 500 to 700 employees in each department. I arranged the information for all the departments I serviced into special files, where I could easily access them. My background in the clerical field was a huge benefit for me because I knew how to organize an office and filing system. In my credenza, I organized all the contracts and supplemental agreements for my departments, so if anyone called regarding a contract issue, I had all the information at my fingertips. I also set up files for grievances, recruitments, leave of absence requests, FMLA, and more. All my weekly and monthly reports were saved on my computer under specific files. Everything was filed and labeled accordingly. This was important. When dealing with large amounts of paperwork, it can't just sit on your desk. All the documents had to be filed away in an organized manner, so if my manager asked for a document regarding a process, I could put my hands on it right away and know the status. When everything is organized properly, you can proceed to planning your time.

STEP TWO: *Time Management*

Many of us have taken time management courses, but until you get a fast-paced job, time management may not be important. Now that I had a fast-paced, demanding job, I had to prioritize my time because my time was precious. At the end of the day, I reviewed my schedule for the next day. Sometimes I would have a meeting first thing in the morning at another location. I didn't want to show up at the main office when I was supposed to be somewhere else. I looked at my planner and reviewed whether I had any meetings that day, so I could plan accordingly.

Knowing your schedule is important. Planners, whether on your phone or tablet, can assist with keeping track of your personal and professional schedules. Reviewing your schedule every morning and evening is key because you may easily forget that you have meetings scheduled throughout the day. After reviewing your schedule, you can prioritize your day. I prioritized the top ten assignments I needed to complete that day. I wrote a list and kept it on my desk. As I accomplished the assignments on my list, I drew a line through each one, indicating it was done. In my line of work, the day didn't always go as planned. Sometimes priorities changed, which meant unexpected situations could occur that need undivided attention. In those cases, I dropped everything and focused on that situation. Afterward, I returned to my planned schedule.

Be prepared for your day to not go as planned and make the necessary adjustments.

As I organized my documents and assignments, I prioritized them according to the timeline in which they had to be completed. Keep your calendar with you at all times. That way, whether you're in the office or at another location, you'll have your schedule at your fingertips. It's a time saver. You may be at a meeting, and it's decided to continue the meeting another day. If you have your planner or calendar with you, you can schedule your meeting right there on the spot.

STEP THREE: *Delegate*

I had to learn to delegate because I was accustomed to doing everything myself. You can't do everything yourself; you need help. Know your resources and available tools and use them. I gave assignments to my office assistant, even though I knew she had other responsibilities. We all did, but she was there to assist me with my assignments as well. She scheduled my interviews and recruitments and sent out all my correspondences for regular processes. If my customers had any payroll issues, I assigned it to the payroll clerk for investigation. Once you delegate an assignment, give that individual a deadline and follow up. Always thank your support team after the assignment is complete. Delegation has many benefits. It frees your time, opens opportunity for sharing responsibilities, and allows other employees to feel trusted. It's a win-win for everyone.

STEP FOUR: *Setting Limits*

You must set limitations. You can't work nonstop without breaks or lunch. You must have time for yourself in your workday. I started out not taking lunches and working through breaks. By 2:30 p.m., I was drained and exhausted. I had headaches, and my brain would shut down from overload. You must recharge your body and brain. Walk away from your work area and take your lunch and breaks so you can rejuvenate your body and mind. Take a walk and meditate. Afterward, you will think and feel better.

My former manager played a nature CD with sounds of chirping birds and flowing water in her office with the doors closed. It was soothing and relaxing. If I closed my eyes when stepping into her office, it felt like being in a beautiful park and sitting by a flowing stream. That worked for her. Do what works for you. The result is the same—less stress.

One of our HR colleagues assigned to the recruitment division was the hardest individual to reach because of his workload. One day, I saw him at lunch, and I thought, *This is my chance to ask him about my recruitment.* He told me very nicely that he didn't discuss work on his lunch break. I understood because you must draw a line and say no when necessary.

STEP FIVE: *Networking*

Networking is the exchange of information among individuals. It is a huge benefit when working for a large company with many departments. It's great to meet and mingle with other colleagues who can assist you with your job assignments. We had several divisions in HR such as employment services, benefits, labor relations, policies, and organization development. If I needed legal advice, I contacted our policies division or the law department. Use the resources around you. They are valuable. This is how you build contacts and relationships. Don't try to reinvent the wheel when there is a process in place or individuals with exceptional knowledge who can assist you. Learn all your resources, pick your colleagues' brains, and gleam from the experience of others. You may also search similar career sites and join organizations to gain more information. Work smarter not harder.

Transition Complete!

Six months of intense training had passed, and I had to battle through some days. Many times, I felt weary and thought maybe I should go back to my previous job. When I felt like that, I immediately encouraged myself and said, "That's not an option. This is what you've been waiting for, and you can't turn around now," and I proceeded to push my way through. A quote from Colin Powell describes my feelings best: "A dream doesn't become reality through magic, and it takes sweat, determination, and hard work." Sweat, determination, and hard work—three things a complacent person doesn't want to hear. You can't be complacent and make your dream a reality. Developing a strategy that works for you is key.

I had passed my probationary period with good reviews from my manager. All my hard work and perseverance had paid off. Now, I was no longer temporary in the title. HR consultant was my permanent position and new career. I had fought for it and won. I felt such a sense of accomplishment. Whatever you set your heart to do, you can accomplish it. I had discovered my professional calling, and I had accomplished my goal!

CHAPTER 4
PRINCIPLES OF BUSINESS CHARACTER

The principles of business character are paramount in your professional calling. These principles consist of ethical standards, wise practices, and high professional values that will navigate you through your daily business interactions. When these business characteristics are executed properly, they are worth their weight in gold. Character is a person's personality and qualities, but when you place business in front of character, a whole new meaning forms. In the business arena, you want to possess qualities that will enhance and advance your career. You may be new to the business world or seasoned in your profession; either way, acquiring these characteristics will assist you with succeeding in your professional calling.

I've selected several business characteristics that will assist you in obtaining true business character.

#1: Integrity

Integrity is the foundation of business character because it's based on trust, honesty, and morality. It is your guide to show you how to conduct yourself in the business world. Unethical practices and procedures creep into businesses every day; however, you must ensure that, whatever profession you choose, you perform with the utmost integrity. Entrepreneurs and corporate executives know that integrity is a precious commodity. One business executive said he looks for an employee to have intelligence and experience, but if he or she doesn't have integrity, they don't meet his standards. Employers know that gaining a knowledgeable employee they can trust to do the right thing is valuable. Otherwise, the employee may turn on the company with unethical conduct.

After you've gained the position you desire, it's important to familiarize yourself with all the work rules, procedures, and policies of the company or business you own. This will enable you to avoid unwanted and problematic situations. Abiding by all the rules of your workplace is a form of integrity. Business owners should set up work rules and procedures for their employees, even if they only have a few employees. Employees should always have a guide for their expected behavior. Integrity is powerful! It means maintaining a high moral standard with all your business transactions, whether you're being monitored or not. In my career, integrity was huge because we had to ensure that all the processes and procedures were done within full compliance of the contract, HR rules, and, most importantly, the law. If any of those three things were violated, we could've opened ourselves up for grievances and lawsuits.

On one occasion, a director from a large department called and asked me to process out-of-class pay for an employee to work in another position. Once I took down all the information and researched the request, I discovered that the position wasn't in the budget for the department. How could someone work in a position that didn't exist? I called the director back immediately and informed him I couldn't approve his request, and I explained that one only qualifies for out-of-class when there is a position open and available. However, I did give him an option. He could add the position to the budget, post it in the department for all who were qualified to apply, and proceed with a fair and legal recruitment of the position. The most qualified candidate would get the position.

Often, people didn't want to hear about the process and procedures to follow. They were just trying to promote one individual, and it wasn't fair. It didn't matter to them whether it was done ethically or unethically. But as the executor of the process, it mattered to me. I've had to combat unethical requests several times, and I always presented the correct process according to the contract and HR practices. You have to be able to look yourself in the mirror and know that you've held on to your integrity.

After a while, your reputation will supersede you. The directors and executives you work with will respect your principles and know what you will and won't do. Many of them will appreciate your integrity, but others will just tolerate it. That's a good thing because you're maintaining your principles of business character.

#2: Resilient

Unfortunately, as we all know, sometimes things go wrong when trying to get that assignment done. Perhaps you missed a deadline, maybe your project didn't meet its goals, or you just forgot to turn in that important report. Maybe you worked hard on a project and gave it your all but didn't get the recognition you deserved. Or perhaps your business placed a bid but someone else was awarded the contract. Whatever the circumstances are, you must bounce back from the disappointment and frustration. That's why being resilient is so important on our list of business characteristics. As much as we would love for everything to turn out perfectly, it's not going to happen all the time. Resilience means being strong and able to take the blow of defeat. If you feel defeated, down, or bent out of shape, it's time to regroup and recover. There may not be anyone there to encourage or motivate you; that's your assignment. You have to encourage yourself. That's how you become strong, healthy, and successful again. Learn from your defeats in the business world, and know that no situation can hold you down. Always bounce back!

I've had to recover from situations during my career. One time, I was asked to testify in a court case for another HR employee. I thought I could easily do it. All I needed to do was take the employee's file to court and answer a few questions. I had never testified in a court case before, and I didn't quite know what to expect, but I thought it would be a simple task. About an hour before leaving for court, I asked my clerical assistant to pull the employee's file. She handed me two extra-large folders stuffed with tons of documents. It was the biggest personnel file I had ever seen. Normally, the files were one medium-sized folder. When I briefly reviewed the file, I saw that it was full of grievances and lawsuits filed by the employee. There were so many that it was difficult to find the court case in question. I got a call from the attorney assigned to the case. She asked me to ensure that the employee's supervisor would be at court. When I called the supervisor, I found out he was out of the office for the day. I quickly realized the situation wasn't turning out well at all. I wasn't the original HR consultant for the case, and the employee's supervisor, who was knowledgeable about the case, wasn't available.

I proceeded to court where everything got worse. The employee's attorney grilled me on the stand, and I couldn't answer many of the questions.

He finally said, "You weren't involved in this case, were you?"

"No," I answered.

The judge excused me from the stand. I knew we'd lost the case that day, and I was disappointed with my testimony. I felt I hadn't represented my company well at all. I walked back to my car with my head down, feeling horrible about everything that had happened. When I got to my car, a parking ticket was on my windshield. I thought, *Okay, what else is going to go wrong?* I wanted to go home and cry, but I went back to the office. I made up my mind that nothing like that was going to happen to me again.

After that situation, I meticulously prepared for all my court cases. I ensured that all my witnesses, whether supervisors, managers, or employees, were present on the court date. Soon, I was known as the HR consultant who testified well in court cases. In fact, I was complimented on many occasions by attorneys who thought my court testimony was always on point and credible. Instead of kicking me off the stand because I didn't know enough about the case, the attorneys kicked me off the stand because I knew too much about the case. They considered me a viable threat to their cases.

The best part of being resilient is watching yourself bounce back. I know it doesn't feel good to be defeated, but if you can be strong, you will regain your stamina and be successful again. Often, we can learn from our setbacks, but in some instances, the quest you're trying to accomplish may not be meant for you at that time. Remember, no matter how great the defeat, there's always a road back to success. As a successful entrepreneur or business professional, you must maintain the ability to regroup and bounce back after defeat. You will have many defeats as well as successes. It's not about the defeat; it's about the successful rebound.

#3: Respect

Respect in the workplace means treating everyone appropriately. Everyone is due respect, regardless of their role. Your words, tone, and demeanor affect the people you work with. Treating your colleagues and customers with kindness and dignity sets an example for your coworkers and, in turn, you will be treated the same way.

As an HR consultant, I was put into many different situations, and I always treated everyone with respect as every professional should. Handling the grievance process was one of my duties. Often, I met with union presidents and chief stewards about issues they wanted to resolve for the employees. It was their job to represent the employees, and it was my job to represent the company and ensure the employees were being treated properly. However, it was also important that we respected each other. We are people, and we can relate to each other on many levels. Prior to the start of our meetings, I'd have a polite conversation with the union representatives about their family. I'd ask how they were doing and engage in small talk to be friendly. It helped set the tone of the meeting. When I started the grievance hearing, the union presented their case, and we discussed the particulars. There's no need to treat individuals in an offensive manner because you disagree with them. It's okay to disagree or agree respectfully. President Barak Obama once said, "We can disagree without being disagreeable." The important thing is hearing each other out, listening to each other's concerns and showing respect. That's our job as professionals.

One union president I met with informed me that everyone didn't handle themselves quite like I did. He explained that some HR representatives didn't speak to them or said as little as possible during the grievance meetings, which he felt was rude. That is unacceptable. You must treat all your customers with dignity and respect. I always say, "You don't have to like me, but you do have to respect me." It's a basic human right.

Below is a list of the dos and don'ts of respect:

DO
- Be courteous
- Be kind
- Listen
- Watch your words and tone
- Treat others like you want to be treated
- Let others finish speaking before you start speaking
- Respect others' opinions

DON'T
- Insult a coworker or customer
- Be biased against others
- Participate in office gossip
- Make condescending remarks
- Participate in bullying

Your coworkers and customers will feel valued when you treat them with dignity and respect. The results are a more productive workforce and a legacy of high professionalism that thrives in your company.

#4: Motivation

Motivation is a huge component of success. It's the driving force that keeps you moving. Some of us move aimlessly just to get through our day. We're not accomplishing much, and we're not aiming for our goals. Dr. Gertrude Stacks once said, "Busy doing everything and accomplishing nothing." You want to focus your energy on reaching the accomplishments you have planned. When you're motivated, the force of accomplishing your goals moves you from one positive outcome to another.

Communication inspires motivation. In the workplace, you will impart, receive, transfer, and share information. These methods of communication build, shape, and motivate you. Keeping the lines of communication open with your manager, colleagues, and staff is valuable.

Meeting regularly with your manager provides you with positive feedback on your work performance. You need that feedback to stay motivated and moving forward. The feedback may not always be positive, but as long as it's constructive, it will help you accomplish your goals and tasks.

Use all constructive feedback as motivation. Meeting with your manager regularly aids in the comfort of having an accessible relationship. Meeting with your staff or team is important, and providing them with feedback on their performance will encourage and motivate them. When you're communicating effectively, you're keeping up with the flow of your organization and maintaining your aspirations.

Here are three powerful words that I call my motivators: Passion, Promise, and Purpose. **Passion** is an indicator that you've found your professional calling. You must be passionate about your career or business. When you're passionate about something, you absolutely love it. You're devoted to it and good at it. No matter how tough things get, telling yourself this is the career you love and dreamed of will help you get through any obstacles that come your way. It's like a shot of adrenaline that keeps you motivated and on the right track. Whatever it takes to accomplish your goals, you're willing to do it. The time at work usually goes by quickly when you're involved in what you're doing. Passion shines through in your attitude, disposition, and behavior because you'll always be willing to go that extra mile to accomplish the task. Your coworkers and colleagues will notice the difference between you and an unmotivated employee. Often, completing a task or assisting a customer will put a smile on your face. Keep that passion flowing for your career, business, and future.

The **promise** is what you've pledged to do. When you started out, you had a plan for your business or career. You may have written it in your journal or shared it with someone you trust. You made a promise to yourself about where you want to go and how you want to get there. Don't break your promise. Stay motivated and complete it. A promise is a declaration, giving the person to whom it was made a right to expect or claim the performance of a specified act. You have the right to claim the performance you must give to be successful. Claim it. It's yours. You've already spoken it. You've made the declaration. Now perform it. Breaking your promise to yourself is a gateway to breaking promises to others, which can't be tolerated in the business world because your credibility is on the line. Take responsibility for your journey and keep your promise to yourself. William Shakespeare said, "To thine own self be true." You must be true to yourself before you can be true to others. Allow your promise to guide you down your career path.

Purpose is what you were meant to do with your life. The career that you have chosen is linked to your purpose. You may have a business that provides a service or you may be a registered nurse who cares for the sick. Whatever your career choice is it can be rewarding, fulfilling, and allow you to be a productive part of the community, giving you the satisfaction of knowing you're making a difference. Your purpose is also your vision for your future. Your professional calling could start off with an entry-level position, while your eyes are on the top managing position. Or perhaps you've started a small business; however, you can see a large business in the making. This is your vision. Always aim high, and never forget your purpose.

Another method of maintaining your motivation is to always remember the whys. *Why am I doing this?* Because I love my career. *Why am I here?* Because this is my professional calling, and I have the gift to excel in it. *Why am I working so hard?* I'm working hard to be successful and financially stable. Keep the whys in the forefront of your mind, and you will remain motivated. Stay focused on your career. Don't become complacent on the job. Some professionals write inspirational notes and leave them in key places, so they can read them every day as a force of influence that keeps driving them forward.

Life brings many ups and downs. Learn how to balance them. Keep your focus on your goals and dreams, even though the big picture may not emerge that day or month. Accomplishing each task and assignment is part of getting you there. Stay motivated.

#5: Leadership

The old saying "In order to be a good leader, you must first be a good follower" is true. To lead, you must know how to follow. If you don't get that experience, you won't be a well-balanced and effective leader. You must learn to be under someone else and serve them well before others can serve you. It gives you a broad perspective of both roles. When you walk in the shoes of a follower, it prepares you to walk in the shoes of a leader. A leader is strong, fair, compassionate, and loyal. Possessing the character of a leader takes patience.

The following prerequisites to leadership will assist you in gaining leadership character in the workplace. When you complete them, you are ready for a leadership position.

STEP 1 - *Be a Good Follower*

A good follower is conscientious and pays attention to the details of their assignments. These individuals always obey the instructions from their supervisors that support the company's principles and policies, even if they don't agree. It shows respect. Sometimes, when someone tells us what to do, we tend to have our own thoughts about the way we should handle the task. Learn to follow instructions. Of course, we expect our managers and supervisors to know all the policies and procedures, but a good follower knows them as well and stays within compliance. A good follower is dependable and reliable. It's important to a company to have employees they can count on. When your manager gives you an assignment, he or she should have full confidence that you're going to complete that assignment in an efficient manner. Having a good reputation of being responsible and dependable is key to building your leadership skills.

In your current role, you will have opportunities to lead. You may not have staff reporting to you, but you can use every aspect of your job to prepare yourself for a great leadership position. Right now, you may have clients or customers who are depending on your guidance and advice to assist them through the services you're providing, and that takes leadership. Leadership is stepping up to the task, being confident, decisive, and creative. Don't be afraid to put your ideas out there. When attending group meetings with your manager or supervisor, if you have a suggestion that will enhance a process, take the opportunity to speak up.

I was at a meeting once, and I mentioned that one of the orientation books was outdated. The managers didn't know about it because most of them didn't handle the orientation process. Later, I was asked to work with one of the HR executives to update the manual. It was a great experience for me, working side by side with such a knowledgeable individual.

During this phase of your learning, it's a good time to take as many management/supervisor training courses as possible. Most employers have a training and development division that offers a variety of courses to teach you how to interact professionally with other employees and prepare you for leadership roles. Take advantage of all the professional training available to you. Employers usually offer excellent training for first-time supervisors or leaders.

STEP 2 – *Leadership Assignments*

One of the first assignments I had as a new HR employee was the orientation process, which is now called the onboarding process. My task was to acclimate new employees who were hired in. I was given an orientation manual and all the associated materials for the session. Everything was laid out and prepared. All I had to do was follow the agenda, right? No. When facilitating to a group of people, you must be familiar enough with the information to answer any related questions. You don't want to read all the information from the manual because that's boring. I used talking points on each subject and elaborated further on the topics. Sometimes, the orientation class ranged from twenty to eighty new hires. I had to be prepared for a small class or a large one. Facilitating is a good starting point when acquiring leadership skills. You are controlling the agenda and the talking points and leading the session. All eyes are on you for the next move. The same is true for a meeting with a few people. It's just a smaller group but the same principle. If you've never facilitated a group or a small meeting, it will bring out your leadership skills. I suggest you start with the meeting first and work your way up to facilitation. After a few sessions, I got the hang of things and put my personal spin on the orientation, making the session informative, interactive, and fun. In the process, I learned leadership skills.

On another occasion, I was asked to assist an employee on a process she was having difficulty learning. The employee had been to training, and she had a huge manual regarding the process, but the process still didn't sink in for her. I knew the process, so I agreed to train her. I went the extra mile and developed a small manual for her that cut through all the red tape of the larger manual and got right to the meat of the process. I sat down with her and went step by step through the process. When we were done with the training, she had a good understanding and didn't have any problems afterward. A leader should be able to train or teach others. It shows that you can impart relevant information to another individual. It takes patience and, in turn, you gain a knowledgeable employee.

Down the line, I developed training manuals for employees in different departments and conducted countless training sessions. I also wrote course descriptions, course outlines, and compiled the associated materials for various training classes. You may start off small in one area, but it can lead to more extensive skills. You must step up to the task and allow your skills to develop. You learn to lead by taking one step at a time.

Volunteer for roles in your company where your leadership skills can be fine-tuned. Don't always wait to be asked. If your company is soliciting for volunteers and you're interested, speak up and offer your services. Good examples of volunteer assignments are employee incentive programs, project management, process improvement teams, and training courses. Employee incentive programs are a lot of fun. You'll have the opportunity to boost employee morale and be a part of a great team. Take on small assignments and work your way up to the bigger ones. The more you volunteer and complete your assignments, the more confident you will be to take on more difficult tasks. These groups are great to work with and will teach you how to interact in a small group where everyone has the same goals. Leading a team like this will ignite your leadership skills. Management is always improving processes and seeking out teams in their organization to step up to the plate and update, revise, and improve their current processes. Because you are familiar with the processes, you can offer your expertise and become a subject matter expert for the team. If your manager wants to assign a task to a project management team, be the first to volunteer for a role on the team. When you're given an assignment, don't do only the minimum. Go the extra mile.

STEP 3 - *Standing in for a Leader*

Some of the best leadership experience I acquired was from working in place of my manager when he or she was off work. Everyone must take a vacation. Managers will need someone to stand in for them at meetings or perform other duties while they're away. Some managers rotate their employees to stand in for them, so all the employees will have an opportunity to gain experience. Or they may opt to use the most experienced employee to fill in for them. It's possible that the manager will ask for a volunteer. Whatever the case, the experience you'll gain is worth the sacrifice it takes to accomplish the duties.

I started out attending meetings for my manager. It was a great opportunity for me to attend upper management meetings I wouldn't normally be invited to. The general manager conducted the meetings, and it gave me a good example of how managers conducted themselves, presented information, and dealt with various situations within their operations. I also presented information on behalf of my manager and answered any associated questions.

At one meeting I attended, my manager asked me to pose a question to the group of managers, and it wasn't an easy one. An employee who didn't have a good work record wanted a transfer, and I asked the group if anyone was willing to take the employee into their department. The room grew painfully silent. Everyone stared at me. I thought, *Why would my manager ask me to do this?* To break the silence, I said, "Going once, going twice ... Gone!" Everyone laughed including me. It was a wonderful ice breaker that allowed me to rebound. I had turned an awkward and uncomfortable situation into a more relaxed environment while completing the task my supervisor had given me.

At another meeting, one of the attendees whispered to me, "Manager in training." I smiled on the inside because I knew that others noticed me while handling my manager's duties.

On many occasions, I was assigned as the lead HR consultant on staff when my manager was on vacation or out of the office. As the lead, I supervised the entire HR office and field operations while my manager was out. It was quite a bit of work, and I didn't get compensated for it. Compensation usually occurred after thirty days, and my manager was never out that long. But the training and experience was worth its weight in gold. I supervised all the HR staff and reviewed their assignments. If any issues came up regarding the staff or the services we provided, I was the go-to person. I was in training for a leadership position and handling everything well.

STEP 4 – *Leadership Role*

There may be times when an opportunity for more responsibilities comes along but it isn't associated with a promotion. Having the duties and responsibilities of a supervisor or lead employee is an opportunity for growth, development, and acquisition of leadership skills. During these opportunities, you must weigh your options carefully and decide what's best for your career. My next major training role for leadership was an assignment change. I was transferred to another location, where I was the lead HR consultant full-time and considered a division head by the department I serviced. It gave me the freedom to manage my own division, and it was a big boost to my leadership journey. I supervised the human resources and payroll division staff, which consisted of six employees. It was a busy office full of challenges, but I loved working there. I attended all the executive staff meetings and presented information about my division. I also provided feedback regarding any HR functions that were in process. This was a perfect setup to lead me into a manager's position. During this assignment, I was selected to interview for a manager position and later offered the job.

Everyone's leadership journey is different, but you must first learn to follow. Following gives you a vivid understanding of the entire spectrum of what you're dealing with as a leader. If you have never been in your employees' position, it will be difficult to understand them and even more difficult to interact and guide them. You gain knowledge and experience from working in both capacities, which will benefit you in the long run. Working in both roles sets the stage for you to be a great leader.

#6: Confidence

If you don't believe in yourself, no one else will. When you walk into the interview to get the job of your dreams, confidence must surround you. You must possess self-assurance and believe that you can do it. During my interview for the HR consultant position, I was calm, *confident*, and articulate. When you have control over yourself, it's called self-possession. I aced the interview because I believed in myself. That doesn't mean I wasn't prepared for the interview. To the contrary, I was very prepared, and that was where my confidence came from. I knew I had studied, and I was equipped to respond to any question. I constantly told myself I was going to be successful in my career, and I was. You must have faith in yourself and believe that you can accomplish the task set before you. Your education, training, and experience give you that confidence.

I'll share an experience I had with one of my customers. A supervisor found a threatening message from her employee. She called her manager in as a witness, took pictures, and documented the event. The information was then submitted to HR. We met with the employee, who admitted responsibility but said the threat wasn't intended for the supervisor. After a thorough investigation, the employee was disciplined and moved to another site to keep the supervisor safe. The employee filed a grievance, and after the fourth-step hearing, the labor relations representative talked to the supervisor, manager, and me. She informed us that we didn't have a case and the discipline we'd issued was too severe. She also warned that if the union went to arbitration, we would lose, and everything would be expunged from the employee's record. The manager and the supervisor grew quiet, and I told the labor relations rep that I disagreed with her about the merits of the case. I spoke up confidently and shared my opinion. The rep's final note was that it was our decision to settle the case now or proceed to arbitration. If we settled the case and reduced the level of discipline, the employee would have the right to return to her original worksite with the supervisor.

I stood on the stairs with the supervisor and manager. The supervisor looked perplexed. "I can't work in this type of environment," she said. "That employee wants to cause me harm."

The manager asked, "What should we do, Ms. Rudolph? Should we just settle the case now and reduce the suspension or risk losing everything?"

I looked at them both intently. "We are not going to settle this case. We're going to arbitration, and we're not going to lose. We're going to win." I was confident that I had enough evidence to win the case. I had faith that I had conducted a thorough and complete investigation with evidence to support our actions. When you're confident about your profession and how well you perform, obstacles that seem huge to others are minimal to you. The supervisor and manager agreed to take my advice, and we proceeded to arbitration.

Our hearing finally came. The arbitrator assigned to our case had a reputation of siding with the union. Nonetheless, I knew we had enough evidence on our side to win. The union requested that the witnesses be sequestered. I disliked being sequestered because we couldn't hear the entire case. It was done so the witnesses would testify independent of each other. I was the first witness. My job was to lay the foundation of the case. The LR rep and I had already discussed our strategies for showing the employee's history during my testimony.

The union rep asked me, "What did your investigation entail?"

That was the worst question for him to ask a person who was as prepared as I was. I took my time, and I laid out my investigation. I was so detailed, in fact, the union rep tried to stop me.

"Excuse me," I said. "You asked me a question about my investigation. This is a very serious question, and it's important to me since I conducted the investigation. I would like to continue." I looked at the arbitrator, and he agreed to let me proceed.

My LR rep gave me a look that said, "You got this." I could see that the LR rep who didn't think we could win the case was now rejuvenated by my testimony. I methodically explained everything about my investigation and how it supported the disciplinary action we'd taken.

Everything was put into evidence, all the paperwork of the investigation, company and department policies and procedures, and the employee's history. The supervisor and manager testified as well. Of course, the employee's union recommended that the discipline be rescinded and the employee be returned to the former job site and position.

It took about eight weeks for the arbitrator to reach a decision. I received the call from the labor relations representative. "You won the arbitration!" she said.

The manager and supervisor were grateful. I gained respect and recognition from Labor Relations and the customers. After a few more cases with similar outcomes, I was even more confident in my abilities.

> *"Through my education, I didn't just develop skills. I didn't just develop the ability to learn, but I developed confidence."*
> – MICHELLE OBAMA

#7: Excellence

Excellence links all the business characteristics together, which is why it concludes the list. Integrity, resilience, respect, motivation, leadership, and confidence all lead to excellence in your professional calling. Excellence means possessing superior skills, high-quality job performance, exceptional attendance, and a positive attitude.

Acquiring superior skills is accomplished through education and training. The training for my career was intense. What I didn't learn from others, I was determined to learn on my own. You must be fully committed to gaining the skills and mastering all the tasks associated with your career. Once you've accomplished that, you can strive for excellence.

Your commitment leads to a standard of high-quality job performance in the workplace, which means doing your best to complete assignments in a stellar fashion. Whether working solo or with a team, you should be driven to accomplish your goals to the best of your abilities. Let's be clear, high-quality job performance is hard work. It doesn't come easy. But the price you pay leads to a great work ethic, contribution to your profession, and personal satisfaction for a job well done. Your performance reviews will be outstanding, which opens the door for higher compensation. Being compensated well makes going back and doing it all over again worth it.

Equally important is exceptional attendance. Being dependable and reliable builds a reputation of trust. Others can trust and rely on you to get the job done. It also gives you a positive work history, which is critical to your success in any position. Good attendance is equally important to qualify for promotions. Show up on time every day and give it your all.

Sometimes, we don't want to give our all when it comes to our attitude. We may think it's okay to have a bad attitude. Attitude in the workplace is like a citizenship grade in elementary school. You may have received A's on your report card in all your classes but received a D in citizenship. That D reflected your behavior, attitude, and conduct. If you got a star in citizenship, it meant your behavior, attitude, and conduct were excellent. That's the type of rapport we want in the workplace. You can be the best at all the business characteristics, but if you have an unprofessional attitude, you have fallen short of excellence. Having a positive attitude not only compels you to feel better and be more productive, but it also influences and encourages your colleagues.

Excellence must be the standard for which you hold yourself accountable.

It isn't acquired overnight. It takes time and patience to master anything you set out to accomplish. To achieve excellence, I encourage you to follow all the business characteristics. Always aim for excellence in your professional calling and strive to possess an outstanding business character.

There are seven business characteristics. In biblical interpretation, the number seven signifies completeness. With these characteristics, you will be a complete professional package, leading you to success in the business world.

CHAPTER 5
PROFESSIONAL BUSINESS IMAGE

Your professional image tells a great deal about you. It's the way you dress, present yourself, communicate, and interact with others. It's how you speak and articulate your ideas about the company or your business and the services you provide. How you are perceived by others is important, and having the right business persona allows you to make a positive impact on those around you. How you behave, speak, and interact with customers and colleagues exhibits how you carry yourself as a professional. It's your professional style.

Image

Your image is all about you, your personality, skillsets, and appearance. How you dress, conduct yourself, and articulate your words reflects you. In addition to possessing all the traits of business character for your professional calling, you'll need the professional business image that accompanies it. You want the whole package, and you can have it.

As an HR consultant, I've had to prepare for court cases. I dressed in formal business attire, and my cases were well prepared with everything in order. I was experienced and knew exactly what I was doing. Prior to the court hearings, I met with the legal advocate who had worked in his field for years and was well respected for his knowledge and expertise. After we completed our review and prep to present our case, he said, "The way you spoke and prepared for the case reminds me of an attorney. Are you studying law?"

"No," I said.

"You have the persona of an attorney."

I took his observation as a compliment. Later, I found out he had contacted my department and expressed the same observation to them. He submitted a positive review about my work performance, even though I hadn't requested for him to do so. If you exhibit a professional image, your colleagues and customers will take note and convey their admiration to others.

People are turned off when you're in a professional position but don't present yourself as a professional. When you arrive at a business, you expect the receptionist or administrative assistant to greet you in a professional manner, including the way they look, act, and respond to you as a customer.

I had an appointment at a banquet facility once. The banquet hall was nice, right off the river with a beautiful view. When I entered the main lobby, the receptionist was sitting at her desk wearing a belly top. Her attire was unprofessional. Things got worse. We were told the facility had scheduled two appointments at the same time, another group and my group, but my group wasn't on the appointment book. It was an oversight. The facility hadn't written in the appointment. Of course, we had to wait, even though we had an appointment. Immediately, I began to form a negative opinion about the facility. Belly tops are not proper attire for professional offices and forgetting a customer's scheduled appointment is another no-no. As they say, first impressions last. We chose another facility for our event. Your image reflects your business.

Business Dress

People are visual beings. When you enter a room, people see you first. They may not know what your profession is or how intelligent you are; all they see is you, from your head to your toes. Think about the impression you're making. Ask yourself if your appearance is professional. Does your appearance reflect your career? Does your appearance say you're a doctor, attorney, chef, entrepreneur, artist, developer, realtor, engineer, or business executive? Your dress and overall appearance should speak for you and say, "I am a business professional" for whatever your profession is.

"Dress for success" and "Dress to impress" are widely recognized phrases, and they're true. If you're striving to achieve success in your career, dress for it. When I was an office assistant, I dressed and conducted myself like a professional before I got the job of my dreams. Dressing for success is preparation for success, whether you're dressing professionally because you want the career of your dreams or because you already have it. Either way, it leads you to success, so you can't lose by dressing in business attire. Wear the success you believe is coming to you. "Dress to impress" implies the impression you leave on others, which should be distinctive. A distinctive impression leaves a positive mark in the minds of others.

One of the attorneys I worked with was articulate, knowledgeable, well-dressed, and pleasant to work with. She left a positive mark on me. I was impressed with her, and her career was successful. Think about what impression you're leaving on your customers and coworkers. You want to make a positive impression in the workplace.

Your overall appearance and persona can demand others' respect. If you're well-dressed and groomed, people will treat you better, whether you're out shopping or on the job. I was getting on an elevator once, returning from lunch, and a young man said to me, "Ma'am, I like your suit, and your hair is nice, too." He proceeded to hold the elevator door open for me when I got off.

On another occasion, I was presenting information to a group of new hires. At the end of the session, one of the young men came up to me to ask a few questions. He said, "You are so together. The way you facilitated and represented your employer today was great. The way you look and dress is so professional." I thanked him and wrote some information for him on a Post-It note. He said, "Wow, your handwriting is terrible!" It tickled me because my handwriting is bad. I thought, *Next time, I'll just print*. People notice everything, which is why you must always put your best foot forward.

Workplace Dress Policy

The workplace dress policy is a specific guideline for employees regarding attire. Whether you work for a small business or a large corporation, adhere to the workplace dress policy. The way you dress gives your customers a positive or negative opinion about the company you represent. Normally, during the orientation process, a dress policy is provided for all new hires. If you don't receive a copy, ask for it. The dress policy is just as important as the company's rules and regulations. Familiarize yourself with the company's policy, read it thoroughly, and refer any questions to your manager or the human resource office. If you're starting your own business, develop a dress policy for your employees. If you don't provide employees with this information, you risk the possibility of employees showing up for work dressed improperly. You don't want that to happen.

There are consequences for not adhering to the company's dress policy. An employee who violates the policy may be sent home for the day. Disciplinary action such as an oral and/or written warning may be issued or suspension for repeat offences. The severity of the discipline depends on the company's policy.

Consider the culture and style of your company. Workplace dress styles include but are not limited to formal business dress, causal business dress, causal smart dress, and casual dress. When in doubt, choose formal business dress.

Formal Business Dress Examples:

MEN
- Business suit (black, navy, or gray)
- Conservative tie
- White or coordinating shirt
- Coordinating dress shoes and socks

WOMEN
- Business suit: pants or skirt (black, navy, or gray)
- White or coordinating shell/blouse
- Pumps and nylons
- Moderate makeup

When working in the downtown area of a major city, professional business dress is considered the norm. When I worked downtown, suits were everywhere, especially during the busy lunch hour. Tourists stuck out like sore thumbs because they were dressed so casually. Formal business attire is standard for conservative Corporate America; however, some new trends have formed.

Business casual dress is appropriate for companies that encourage a more relaxed workplace. Whether business casual or the more polished formal business attire, employees should always be well-groomed.

Casual Business Dress Examples:

MEN
- Shirt, vest, sweater, sport jacket
- Pants type: dress, khaki, dockers, or corduroy
- Variety of color choices
- Casual shoes, loafers

WOMEN

- Blouse, vest, sweater, jackets
- Pants type: dress, khaki, and linen
- Skirts and dresses
- Variety of color choices
- Open-toe shoes

Inappropriate Workplace Attire

Using good judgement about your work attire is important. If you feel something may not be appropriate for the workplace, it probably isn't. The length of women's dresses and skirts should be at the knee or below. Avoid t-strap dresses, exposed cleavage, high splits, and back-out dresses.

Men and women's pants should be ironed. Don't wear sweatpants, exercise pants, leggings, shorts, capris, or spandex. Avoid jeans unless allowed on an approved dress-down day. Shirts, blouses, and tops should not have any obscene language, pictures, or symbols on them. Don't wear t-shirts, t-strap tops, belly tops, or back-out tops. Do not wear gym shoes, flip-flops, thongs, or slippers. This list doesn't encompass everything, but it is a basic guideline.

Shopping Smart for Your Business Attire

You should first consider your company's dress policy. That will help you decide what to purchase. Both men and women should focus on neutral colors. Start with a foundation of black, taupe, navy, and gray suits or separates such as jackets, skirts, and pants. These colors can be mixed and matched repeatedly. You can add a pop of color with a blouse, shirt, tie, or scarf. Remember to select quality pieces for longer wear.

Landing a great new job that requires business attire when you don't have money to look the part can be an issue. Below are suggestions for all budgets.

FLEXIBLE BUDGET

With a flexible budget, you can shop the discount stores, outlets, and major retail stores. Always look for sales on name-brand clothing. Search for coupons, special buys, or door busters on the retailer's website or sales paper. You may find designer clothes for a fraction of the cost. Take someone with you who has a flare for shopping economically and fashionably. It's always good to have someone else's opinion when making a decision. If all else fails and you can't get anyone to go shopping with you, use your phone and take a picture of yourself in your new business clothes and send it to your friend for a second opinion.

LIMITED BUDGET

If you don't have much money, shop at your local thrift or secondhand stores. Some of them are setup like department stores. Now, it's considered trendy to shop the secondhand stores. The prices are great! I know several friends who have landed executive jobs but didn't have the money to shop at brand-name stores for a new wardrobe. The thrift shop gave them what they needed. I was amazed by some of the clothing they had purchased. When I saw a particular friend, she always had on a nice business suit or coordinating separates. "Don't tell me you got that outfit from the thrift shop, too?" I'd say. But of course, she had. Her jackets, skirts, and suits were nice, name-brand items. The thrift shops give you a large selection at minimum cost. Look for new or slightly worn suites and jackets. Browse several shops and make wise choices. Some shops have additional discounts on top of the already low prices.

Another acquaintance was promoted to a management position, and the dress policy was khaki pants and navy shirts. He had a limited budget, and I suggested the secondhand store. He purchased everything he needed for his new job at the Good Will. He bought four pair of khaki pants. Some were brand name like Ralph Lauren and Calvin Klein. Some of the shirts were brand new, and many of the items were half off.

One of the employees I serviced was a truck driver. When I met her, she was wearing denim overalls. She had suffered an injury on the job, and the company was moving her to a light-duty position. I had an open position for a receptionist that she could work temporarily. When I mentioned the position to her, she said she didn't have clothes for a job like that. Her wardrobe consisted of jeans and overalls.

"You don't have any dresses, skirts, or dress pants?" I asked.

She said, "I only have my 'get a man' outfit that I wear to the club." She was dead serious!

I didn't ask her to describe the outfit, but it sounded inappropriate for the office. I gave her some of the above suggestions, and the next time I saw her, she was dressed nicely in a professional blouse and dress pants. She liked the temporary job so much that she didn't want to go back to truck driving. It feels good to dress nice. Of course, she had to go back eventually, but the temporary position motivated her to think out of the box. Perhaps she could train truck drivers or work in management. I love when a person's creative juices flow about their career and potential for the future.

NO BUDGET

Ask relatives or friends if they have jackets or suits they don't wear. It doesn't hurt to inquire. Usually, family and friends don't mind helping out for a new job. Also, consider contacting non-profit organizations that assist job seekers with appropriate business attire. These organizations are there to aide disadvantaged job seekers with the resources they need. Below are a few websites:

www.dressforsuccess.org

www.jacketsforjobs.org

www.thebridgetosuccess.org

Résumé

When applying for a job, the first thing the recruiter or manager sees is your résumé. It doesn't take long for them to realize it isn't well written. Your résumé is your introduction to the job market, and it reflects you. A professional, well-crafted résumé is a must when you seek to gain the attention of a prospective employer, even if you already work for the company to which you're submitting your résumé and you want to move up in the ranks. Your résumé can shed light on skills and abilities your current employer didn't know you possessed. It is an integral part of your professional image.

RÉSUMÉ BUILDING TIPS

- Your résumé should be organized and well written.
- Include a header, summary statement, skills and technology, education, and work experience.
- You may include non-paid internships, volunteer work, and course work.
- Have someone else proofread for typos and grammatical errors.

DOS & DON'TS OF RÉSUMÉS

- Do use bullet points in the body. It helps to focus on your qualifications.
- Do keep it under two pages. You don't want to deter recruiters or managers because your résumé is too long.
- Do include measurable work accomplishments.
- Do update your résumé with key words from the job description that you are applying for because recruiters look for some of those key words.
- Don't send out the exact same résumé for all the positions you apply for. Customize each one for the position.

- Don't have outdated information or outdated skillsets on your résumé. Make sure all the information is correct and the listed skillsets reflect current technology.
- Don't list an unprofessional email address (ex: partydown@gmail.com) or a phone number with an unprofessional voicemail greeting. You don't want to give prospective employers the wrong impression.

Always remember to send a cover letter with your résumé, whether it's requested or not. Don't send a generic cover letter. Customize it to fit the job you're applying for. If you need additional assistance with your cover letter and résumé, please contact Faith Thompson at www.savvycareerseeker.com.

Social Media

Your social media image is just as important as your real-life persona. What type of image are you giving others on social media? Some employers visit the social media accounts of perspective employees to find out what they're really doing.

According to a recent CareerBuilder survey, employers are monitoring job candidates on social networking sites. Research shows that seventy percent of employers are using social networking sites to find out more about job candidates. Additionally, fifty-seven percent of employers found inappropriate behavior that caused them not to employ the candidate (CareerBuilder, 2019).

According to the article, employers consider the following on social networking sites:

- Does the candidate have a professional image
- Posts that others make about the candidate
- Reasons not to employ the candidate
- Validation of the candidate's resume

Make sure the image you project on social networking sites is appropriate for the career you want. Clean up your social media sites by removing all inappropriate posts and images. Your reputation and professional image are important. If you need help with this, there are companies that will assist you with the clean-up process.

Balance

Embrace all the components of your professional career, not just one or two. Look the part and act the part. Possess all the traits of business character, and have the professional image that goes with it. I know some talented and gifted business people, but their appearance doesn't match up to those qualifications. I also know individuals who have a professional appearance and are talented in many areas, but their personality and bad attitude taint their gifts and abilities. You must have balance. If you only have part of the package, you will come up lacking. When you walk into a room, carry the whole package. That's balance!

CHAPTER 6
MASTER YOUR SOFT SKILLS

Soft skills are a combination of interpersonal people skills, social skills, communication skills, character traits, attitudes, career attributes, social intelligence, and emotional intelligence quotients among others that enable people to effectively navigate their environment, work well with others, perform well, and achieve their goals with complementing hard skills.

("SOFT SKILLS," 2019)

The above definition explains every component of this precious commodity in a nut shell. Some business professionals are known for their soft skills, how well they handle people, problem solve, and manage difficult situations. Others are known for not having soft skills, which limits their ability to grow and develop positive relationships.

People Skills

People skills are an asset in the workplace. It's the human part of us, our sensitive side. As a business professional, people skills are just as important as hard skills. Hard skills are the foundation of your career: your education and training and all the technical experience you've acquired for your career. However, people skills enhance hard skills through effective communication, teamwork, problem solving, and many other attributes. Our soft skills must show through in our day-to-day interactions. When you have people skills, you know how to handle people, making it easy for you to interact with them, even in unpleasant situations. These skills can be learned through training and development courses that many corporations offer to their employees.

People skills consist of knowing how to listen, understanding others, being patient, exhibiting good judgement, and the ability to negotiate. I had received a call from an employee who had been informed that her leave of absence request had been denied. This employee wasn't in my service group, so my team didn't deny her leave; it was processed by another team. After the employee introduced herself, she asked me to listen to her story, even though she knew I wasn't her HR representative. I agreed to hear her out. I listened carefully and asked her some questions. She asked if I could assist her with the situation. I informed her that I understood how she felt, but I couldn't promise her anything since another team had handled her request. She softly said that she understood and thanked me for listening to her.

Her call troubled me because I knew if I would've processed her leave request, I would've approved it. She met all the HR requirements. I had to make a judgement call: allow the employee to be denied a benefit she was eligible for or intervene on her behalf. I chose the latter and decided to talk to the HR representative who had denied her request. This particular HR rep wasn't always pleasant to interact with. When I approached her, I started out with small talk before asking about the employee's request. We talked a little more and laughed about some office issues. When I mentioned the employee's name, the HR rep's facial expression changed. It was rare to question another HR rep about how they handled a process. I wasn't her manager, so it was a little tense, but she explained to me in detail why she had denied the request. I listened and didn't interrupt. Afterward, I mentioned that the employee was eligible for the leave and the reason she was requesting was consistent with our policies and guidelines. The HR rep agreed but indicated that she thought the employee could manage the situation without taking a leave from work. That wasn't her call to make. I simply asked her to put herself in the employee's position. A few days later, the employee called me and informed me that her leave had been approved. She was grateful for my assistance. This difficult situation took people skills to resolve. I had patience with the employee and listened to her complaint, even though she was not under my service group. I made a judgement call to intervene on her behave. And I used negotiation skills with the HR rep to yield a positive outcome. I handled both individuals wisely, utilizing my people skills and hard skills to resolve the issue without burning bridges.

Social Skills

As the old saying goes, "Treat others the way you want to be treated." When you treat others well, you acknowledge them and let them know they are important. You do this by being cordial and friendly with your coworkers, customers, clients, and staff. Always maintain a professional but congenial demeanor. Be friendly and speak to everyone. Make eye contact and reach out to shake hands. Learn how to be assertive but not aggressive. Assertion means putting your best foot forward, being confident. Aggressive is confidence too, but it can be perceived as belligerent, combative, or offensive. Knowing how to interact with others and maintaining the integrity of your profession are key assets for all professionals. Some professionals have a reputation for treating others poorly, which offends the ones on the receiving end, like refusing to be a team player or talking down to coworkers.

An HR representative who wasn't part of my team asked me for information for a customer. I gladly assisted her, although I wondered why she didn't ask her own team leader. What she said after I helped her gave me a good understanding. She thanked me for my help and informed me that she couldn't go to her own team leader because the team leader always belittled her and made her feel embarrassed. As she explained, tears swelled in her eyes. If an employee comes to you for advice or information, assist them in a professional manner without belittling them. Possessing good social skills means cooperating with others and working as a team in the workplace.

Effective Communication

Another valuable soft skill is effective communication, which entails sharing, listening, having empathy, giving clarity, keeping an open mind, and providing feedback. But being a good communicator in the workplace isn't always easy. Sometimes, we are so busy trying to complete the task at hand in a timely matter, knowing there are several other tasks to complete, that we can become poor communicators because we're overwhelmed with day-to-day operations. By embracing soft skills, you can be an effective communicator.

We share information constantly in the workplace. Our audience and the type of information we convey determine how we share the information. For instance, you may have a one-on-one meeting with a colleague to discuss a new procedure, or you may meet with your team every morning for five to ten minutes for a brief update on a project. Maybe you're presenting a proposal to customers in the conference room with an agenda, Power Point slides, materials, handouts, and the whole works. Either way, your objective is the same, to share information, collaborate with others, and provide an openness that will create trust and feedback, which will ultimately lead to your goals.

Usually, when I had missed a meeting, I touched base with one of my colleagues for the highlights. Not knowing information can affect your performance. Also, if you're a team leader or manager, it's your job to pass on any information that will assist your team with their assignments.

There was a situation when our manager didn't provide our team with important information that affected the team. Instead, we heard about the information from another team who also informed us that our manager knew about everything well in advance and we should have been advised. The information was bad news and a blow for the team. It made us feel let down by our manager. You don't want a situation like this to happen. Poor communication brings division and harbors mistrust. Filter down information, good or bad, when it affects your team. Everyone should be kept in the loop.

Another part of effective communication is listening. Always hear the other individual out. Never cut them off or rush them. You must possess patience to be a good listener. Even if you've formed an opinion, hold it until they're finished because they may say something that will change your opinion. Make eye contact. Don't look away while the person is expressing themselves. Make sure they have your undivided attention. Watch your body language. Don't fold your arms or flip through paperwork. That sends negative messages to the person who's talking. Stay focused and periodically nod so the individual who's speaking will be confident that you're hearing them. If you need to ask a question for clarity, wait for a break in the conversation. Feedback shows you're listening and you're seeking clarity.

I was servicing a department I loved working with, and my manager informed me that she was transferring me to another department. It wasn't uncommon to be transferred to another group. Two weeks later, I was at my new department, and I received a call from one of my former customers at the old department, complaining about the new person who had taken my place. He said, "The new HR representative doesn't listen to me. When I talk to her, she's always rushing me off the phone. You always listened to me and answered all my questions. I wish you would come back and be our HR representative again." I told him to give the new HR rep some time to adjust to the new assignment. Customers want to be heard. They want to know if you understand their concerns and are willing to assist them. People love to be treated well!

Always show empathy. Let the individual know you understand how they feel. In most cases, just having someone listen to you and understand how you feel can bring relief. Empathy shows that you care and you can connect with the feelings of others, which is a soft skill that's necessary in the workplace. I had a grievance hearing with the chief steward and the president of the association. The case was about an employee who had worked in a higher position for a period of time. According to the grievance, the employee's department had promised her compensation, but she never received it. The union presented documentation. After reviewing everything, I said, "Allow me to further investigate the grievance, and if the evidence shows that the employee did work in the position and didn't get compensated, I will grant your grievance." They were stone faced, and silence filled the room because they were shocked that I cared enough to further investigate on behalf of the employee. Usually, the grievance would be denied all the way up to arbitration, and the employee would have to wait all that time to be properly compensated. But I understood how the employee felt because I had been in the same situation many years earlier. You want someone to care when you've been treated unfairly. After my investigation, I discovered that their concerns were true, and I granted the grievance. The employee was fully compensated. Afterward, the president of the union always treated me with the upmost respect. Empathy in the workplace is strength.

Emotional Intelligence vs. Social Intelligence

> *"If your emotional abilities aren't in hand, if you don't have self-awareness, if you are not able to manage your distressing emotions, if you can't have empathy and have effective relationships, then no matter how smart you are, you are not going to get very far."*
> —DANIEL GOLEMAN

Having the ability to understand and care about the feelings of coworkers, subordinates, customers, and friends is part of emotional and social intelligence, soft skills that are necessary for the workplace. Emotional intelligence (EI) focuses on our feelings. Learning self-awareness can help manage your personal feelings. People who understand themselves can better understand others. Social intelligence

(SI) focuses on being sensitive about other people's emotions and feelings, which enables you to develop a rapport with others that fosters a positive relationship. EI deals with the inside of you, and SI deals with your outside world. As professionals, embracing EI and SI helps us maneuver through our day-to-day activities and positively influences our decision-making skills. Emotional and social intelligence also aide in problem solving and conflict resolution because you can understand the feelings and concerns of others.

One of my colleagues was meeting with an employee who he indicated was difficult to talk to. The employee had issues at his job site that he wanted to discuss with human resources. My colleague asked me to attend the meeting to assist, and I agreed. During the meeting, I initiated the conversation with the employee and listened carefully to his complaint. I could see that he was upset about the situation, and I understood how he felt and why he felt that way. That is a part of emotional intelligence. I sympathized with him. I gave him the best remedy for his situation, and I took my time explaining it to him. He was agreeable to my suggestive resolution. We had a good outcome, and I had no problems with the so-called difficult employee. I left my colleague with him to work out the logistics of our agreement, and my colleague informed me that as soon as I left the room, everything started falling apart. People know when you care about them and have empathy for their situation. Your concern must be genuine, or they'll have difficulty communicating with you. Soft skills are the key to empowering your hard skills.

CHAPTER 7
YOUR GIFT WILL MAKE ROOM FOR YOU

"A man's gift maketh room for him, and bringeth him before great men" (Proverbs 18:16 KJV). I love this scripture because it's for everyone. All of us were born with a gift, and that gift can be linked to your career and professional calling. Let's rephrase the scripture: A man's calling makes room for him. When you discover and embrace your calling, the opportunity for advancement will be presented to you. But it starts with your determination to believe, move, grow, and develop the calling within you. The second part of the scripture says, "And bringeth him before great men." This could refer to corporate, business people, wealthy people, and people who believe in you, men and women with power and influence who see great potential in you. These individuals will notice your gift and advance you because of it.

Next are the stories of individuals who followed their heart and leaped into their professional callings.

Deborah, *former dean of health sciences*

Deborah was an occupational therapist for many years, and it was a great career. She enjoyed treating her patients and assisting them with their recovery. Deborah especially enjoyed working with and training students for her profession. She had years of clinical faculty experience, which enabled her to train students from various colleges and universities. However, Deborah had a desire to teach students in the classroom at the college level. She was unable to pursue her dream due to family issues, so she had to put it on the back burner, and after a while, she began to think it was too late for a career change. However, while at a church service one evening, her pastor, Dr. Gertrude Stacks, prayed for her and said: "There are people you occasionally go around, and you don't think much about it, but you should go around them more often. I see a graduation cap on your head, and you have to pass the class of education."

Afterwards, Deborah started networking with her colleagues more regularly and attending association meetings. There, she met therapists who worked at colleges, and she asked them if openings were available and to keep her in mind if anything opened part-time or full-time. However, it was a known fact that it was difficult to get a teaching or faculty position. One day, one of her colleagues sent her an email, stating that a full-time faculty position for an occupational therapist was available at her college and to apply if interested. At first, Deborah hesitated because she had been at her current job for many years, and she was comfortable. It was easy, she had seniority, and she enjoyed the people. There were many reasons to stay, yet she knew it was time for a change. She spoke with Dr. Stacks, and she encouraged Deborah to apply for the position, advising her that this was her opportunity to move into the position God wanted her to have. The college scheduled her for an interview. She was nervous because she hadn't been on a job interview for more than a decade. She planned mock interviews with family and friends to prepare for the process. The day of her interview, she met with approximately six academic faculty members, administrators, and college presidents. Afterward, she felt the interview went well.

In her role as a therapist, she treated various patients with physical and developmental disabilities. She dressed casually because of the type of work she did, but now it was time to move on to her calling, and that meant dressing in business attire. A short time after her interview, she received a call from the college, offering her the position.

Leaving her occupational therapist position, where she had worked for many years, was difficult because the staff and patients were like family. Deborah turned in her resignation and went to her car in the parking lot and cried, but she knew that, even though she would miss everyone, she had made the right decision.

Teaching at a college was a huge transition for Deborah because she had entered the field of higher education, but she knew God had opened that door for her, and she was excited about her new career path. She didn't mind stepping out into uncharted waters.

After she had been teaching at the college for a while, some of the programs were abruptly revamped. The changes affected the program for which Deborah was teaching, and she had no idea what would happen to her. The college could offer her another position, or they could let her go. One of the college presidents with whom Deborah had worked submitted a favorable recommendation on her behalf to the chancellor of the college. She informed Deborah, "I told the chancellor, 'Whatever you do, you must keep Deborah here at the college.' "

After the recommendation, the chancellor and the president held a meeting with Deborah, and he said, "I value the opinion of this president, and she thinks highly of you and believes you will be an asset to this college. I am impressed with that; therefore, I plan to appoint you as district dean of health sciences and careers, and you will be a part of my executive board. Your office will be down the hall from mine."

Deborah was shocked but thankful that she had followed Dr. Stacks' advice. During the commencement ceremonies at the college, Deborah wore the graduation cap that Dr. Stacks had seen when she prayed for Deborah. Now, her new role involved working with health professionals such as nurses, dental hygienists, and surgical technologists. It was a 180-degree turnaround for Deborah.

Deborah's definition of success:

"Keep your eyes on the prize, and you shall succeed."

AUTHOR'S COMMENTARY:

Deborah's situation was unique because she had worked in her field for many years prior to obtaining the promotion to dean. Your professional calling can set you up for a greater purpose. Deborah made a leap from one career to the next when she left her former position and accepted the offer from the college. She found favor with the president and chancellor of the college. Her gift brought her before great men and advanced her to another level. Deborah went from an occupational therapist to an occupational therapist instructor to dean of health careers and sciences. No more casual clothes; suits and pumps are now her professional business attire. Deborah kept her eye on the prize, which led her to a successful career.

Daralynn, *human resources recruiter and author*

After Daralynn graduated from college, she knew she wanted to pursue a career in human resources, specifically recruiting. She enjoyed seeing people get the job of their dreams and assisting them with their career choices. She also loved talking to people about career goals and aspirations. The only obstacle was that Daralynn's degree wasn't in HR, but in communications, which would make it difficult to land an HR recruiting position. Daralynn decided to apply for an admissions recruiter position at a major university, and she got the job. Although it wasn't the HR position she desired, she believed the admissions recruiter position would give her a pathway to a HR career. As an admissions recruiter, Daralynn had the opportunity to work with students from all around the world. She recruited the students and qualified them for admission to the university. She also followed up with them all the way to the first day of class. Although Daralynn enjoyed working with the students, she still yearned for a HR recruiting career.

Over the next six years, Daralynn remained an admissions recruiter while applying for countless positions in HR and being denied. Employers said she was underqualified. They didn't consider her recruiting experience for the college the same as recruiting for a company. Although she possessed stellar skills for dissecting résumés, recruiting students, and interviewing, no one would give her a chance to prove she had the skills of an HR recruiter.

Eventually, Daralynn started working with a job recruiter at a major company. When she had submitted her résumé to the recruiter, she was first offered a finance position, but she expressed her desire to pursue an HR career, and the recruiter decided to help her. The recruiter later called her about an HR internship with the company. It would be a difficult move because she would take a major pay cut. But for Daralynn, it wasn't about the pay; it was about finally getting into the career of her dreams.

When she accepted the HR internship, it was a humbling experience because she was the only one of the interns who had been out of college for six years. The others had just graduated. But she persevered because her goal was to turn her career around. The internship was with one of the best companies in Michigan, and the experience Daralynn gained was a huge blessing to her career. She excelled above everyone because of her previous experience as an admissions recruiter. And now, her experience as an intern put her in a different league from other entry-level HR recruiters. After one year working as an intern, Daralynn got a call from an engineering recruiting firm. They were impressed with her experience as an HR Intern and admissions recruiter. Finally, all Daralynn's experience was lining up for her career. The company hired her as a HR recruiter. The function of the company was to recruit and hire candidates for the engineering field, but Daralynn didn't have any experience recruiting engineers. Her team leader, who was a skilled engineering recruiter, saw Daralynn's potential and trained her through the recruiting and hiring process for engineers. Because of the training and guidance Daralynn received from her team leader, she became proficient in her field. Her team leader became her mentor and friend.

Over the next two or three years, Daralynn was hired by other companies as an HR recruiter, but even though she was excelling in HR, her salary was still low compared to what she had earned as an admissions recruiter. She was eventually interviewed by a global engineering firm and offered a position as an engineering recruiter with an excellent salary. In fact, the position she acquired is one of the most coveted recruitment positions in the firm.

Daralynn now enjoys an abundant salary, a position she can work from home, and, most importantly, the job of her dreams! But Daralynn's story isn't over. Some people have more than one dream inside of them, and that was true for Daralynn. She also had a passion for writing. It started when she was just a child. Her mother was a librarian, and Daralynn was practically raised at the library. That was when she began to read all the books in her age category, and her love affair with writing began. She noticed that out of all the children's books she read, very few were about people of color like her. When she got older, she first decided to write Christian fiction books for teens but later wrote books for African American children because of the void for young girls of color. She started a series for African American girls that includes a host of black characters for children. Her books are positive and fun for African American children everywhere. To accomplish her writing goals, Daralynn got up early every morning before her work day and wrote for at least a half hour. This was a sacrifice because she has a husband and two children, but she was committed to her writing schedule. She did her research, reading numerous children books to learn how to write so children would understand the message she wanted to convey. With much hard work, Daralynn finally finished her book. She was blessed to find a technical staff that believed in the project and assisted her with the editing, illustration, and production.

When Daralynn's book hit Amazon, it sold out not once but twice. Her book is a great success! Her series allows her to travel the country, and she always receives positive feedback from parents and children who love reading her books. Daralynn has managed to have two successful careers going for her at one time. Her HR position is her main job and supersedes even her writing. That's why she rises early in the morning to write what's on her heart and goes on to provide high-quality service as an HR professional for the rest of the work day. Daralynn loves both her careers, and she has learned how to balance them both.

> Daralynn's definition of success:
> *"Being happy mentally and physically in your own space. I'm grateful to be able to create my own work schedule and do the things I love."*

AUTHOR'S COMMENTARY:

Daralynn's career testimony has all the components of faith, hard work, and dedication. Her decision to take the lower-paying internship was a wise and strategic move. However, it took a leap of faith. She was persistent in achieving her goal to become an HR recruiter. Sometimes, you must take a pay cut to rise and excel. This concept is hard for many individuals because everyone just wants to move forward. Daralynn was moving forward, perhaps not in her salary, but in her skills, experience, and abilities. It takes faith to step into a choice like that and belief that it's the right move for you. Daralynn's dedication kept her focused on her outcomes and not her present situation. The decision payed off for her and the outcome was great. While all this was going on for her, she was pursuing another dream to become an author. With much hard work,

Daralynn accomplished all her dreams. In order for your gift to make room for you, you must believe in yourself and what God has placed inside you. Faith is what drives you, and the evidence of faith appears when the doors of opportunity start opening for you. Daralynn's gift made room for her and brought her before people who supported and assisted her with the dreams God put in her heart. Now Daralynn is successful and grateful that she's pursuing the things she loves.

Kwame, *entrepreneur*

Kwame was drawn to the hair industry around the age of seventeen. After having several negative experiences with his barber like waiting for hours to get his hair cut when he was on time for his appointment or his barber constantly putting other customers ahead of him, he was motivated to start cutting his own hair, which was a basic lineup and trim. He proceeded to cut his friends' and family's hair as well. Kwame worked his nine-to-five job during the week, and on the weekends, he cut hair in his garage or bathroom for ten dollars a head.

Everything was going well until his employer fired him. He had a family to support and bills to pay. He had to do something to support his family, and he didn't want to go back to a nine-to-five job. Kwame wanted to be his own boss, making his own decisions, and he didn't want to be in a position where he could be fired again. He decided to cut hair full-time. He enrolled into school to obtain his barber stylist certification. Near the end of the program, a friend of his opened a barber shop and asked him if he would be interested in renting a booth there. Kwame accepted the offer and was eager to start.

During his first week there, he didn't have any customers and rent was due for his booth that Saturday. His friend still expected rent money despite the fact that Kwame hadn't earned any money that week. The situation placed a hustling spirit inside Kwame to find clients for the next week. He called, texted, got on Facebook, and offered promotions and free cuts to potential clients to generate business. And he was successful! He started building clientele and his passion for his profession. Kwame's expertise grew, and he went from an even-steven barber who only cut African Americans' hair to mastering all kinds of savvy styles for any ethnic group.

Kwame worked at his friend's barbershop for a few years. While he was there, he learned about the business, what it took to manage a barbershop, and the importance of providing quality service to clients. There were disadvantages as well. Kwame wanted a professional, family-oriented environment for his customers, and his friend's barbershop didn't provide that. His goal was to eventually own and manage his own shop, so he could create the kind of business environment he desired. He started researching all the aspects of starting his own business, and he learned that it was an expensive investment.

During that time, his pastor, Dr. Stacks, instructed him to start looking for a building because the Lord was going to bless him with his own shop. Kwame didn't follow the instruction because he didn't have the finances or resources to start his own business. He thought, *How can God be telling me to look for a building, and He knows I don't have the money?* A few months later, Dr. Stacks told him again that the Lord said for you to start looking for a building. And again, Kwame didn't follow the instruction. Dr. Stacks inquired about Kwame's business a third time, but this time, she informed him that not only would the Lord give him a building, but He was also going to give him the staff to go with it. Kwame still didn't pursue it. Finally, one Sunday, in front of the entire church, Dr. Stacks asked him, "Have you done what the Lord said?"

Kwame wanted to say yes, but that wasn't the truth. "No," he responded honestly.

She asked Kwame, "If God told you to start a business and go look for a building, why would you worry about money?"

Her question stunned Kwame. He had never told her there was an issue with money, but it was evident that the

Lord had told her. It propelled Kwame to finally start looking for a building.

He told everyone—his friends, family, and clientele—that God was going to give him a building for his business. He found three buildings of interest, and he finally settled on an 800-square-foot storefront. Kwame thought the building would be a good start for him. He met with the landlord and they negotiated the rental fee. The landlord wanted $200 more than what Kwame was willing to pay. But she lowered the price, and Kwame got the keys to his shop that day. He was excited! But reality hit: The shop was empty, and he now had the task of getting equipment and staff for his business.

Every day after work, he went to the shop and prayed. He told God, "Yes, I have the shop, but I don't have any equipment or staff to go in the shop, and I don't have the money to buy equipment." This went on for months. Sometimes Kwame went to the shop, sat, and wept before the Lord. "I did what you told me to do, but I can't go to the left and I can't go to the right. I'm in an empty shop," he said to the Lord.

People began calling Kwame, telling him they'd heard he was opening a shop and they wanted to help him with the project. They asked him what he needed for his shop and donated equipment. Kwame purchased some of the equipment himself, and the vendors dropped the prices so low it was almost a giveaway. His church family also gave donations. God had provided him with everything he needed. The project was complete! He named the shop Anointed Touch, the name he'd wanted since he'd started cutting hair in his garage.

Kwame had a beautiful grand opening for his shop that consisted of a staff of five barbers, including him. During the grand opening, Dr. Stacks looked around and said, "This is very nice, but the Lord said this isn't it."

Her revelation put him in awe and made him feel a great anticipation for something special to happen for him. The shop was his learning ground, and during the first year in business, he had made some mistakes and learned from them. He discovered how hard it was to recruit good staff who wanted to work in a family-friendly environment. Kwame went through many barbers, trying to find the right ones for his shop. During this time, the Lord placed influential people around him. One day, he was sharing with one of his clients his vision for his next shop, and he explained how he wanted a full-service salon that offered barber services, hair stylists, nail technicians, make-up artists, and massage therapy. "But I don't have the money to do it," he added.

His client was impressed with his vision and asked him, "How much would a salon like that cost?"

Kwame gave him a figure, and the client said, "Dude, I got it!" Kwame had an investor for his second shop.

The search was on for the second shop, which had to accommodate a full-service salon. Three months later, he found his shop, a former comic book store that was 3,400 square feet. The building had to be gutted and refinished from the ceiling to the floors. Kwame had to purchase everything for the shop in multiples of ten because of the staff he would hire. He didn't take into account the massive cost of plumbing for such a large building. He soon realized he had underestimated the price of his new project, but that wasn't going to stop him. He gained favor with the plumbing company, and they did the work for the cost of materials only. The new Anointed Touch Salon opened four years to the day of the first shop's grand opening. Now, Kwame owns and manages a full-service salon with a staff of twelve employees.

"Acquiring this building and how God orchestrated everything blew my mind!" he said. Kwame achieved his goals of making his own decisions, being his own boss, and living his dream.

Kwame's definition of success:

> *"My business is growing every day. I'm striving to reach a greater potential in the hair industry. Success to me is being comfortable in every area of my business and life. It's acquiring an inheritance to pass down to my children."*

AUTHOR'S COMMENTARY:

Kwame's testimony embodies the scripture and theme for this chapter. I love how the Lord worked in his life regarding his professional calling. Kwame had to battle himself and his insufficiencies to do what the Lord told him to do. Many of us may not have the finances, skillsets, or resources, but if we are called for a profession, we must step out, regardless of how unqualified we feel because God will give us everything we lack. The Lord wants us to have exactly what He has planned for us, but we must believe and act on what He has given us to do or we will never reach our professional calling.

It was simply miraculous how Kwame obtained both buildings for his business. He didn't spend a lot of his own money. It was given to him. What a blessing! God can send you investors and people who believe in you.

Gina, *director of cardiovascular technology*

Gina had just completed six months of medical assistant training when she landed a position as an EKG technician in noninvasive cardiology at a local hospital. It was her first job in a medical professional setting. The position was part-time, and it was the midnight shift. The EKG technician position was the least esteemed job in the department, but Gina looked at it as a bridge for better things to come. Her goal was to be the best, and to do that, she knew she had to do her best.

Gina knew she had to learn everything about her role and the department in which she worked. She didn't hesitate to be cross-trained or learn new processes or procedures, so she grew quickly. She possessed great enthusiasm for her field, so much so that her superiors took notice and began to coach and train her for an advanced role in cardiac testing.

Gina set the bar high and always held herself to a high standard of work ethic and professionalism. She arrived early for work in polished, professional attire. She never complained and constantly wore a smile. She believed that if she wanted a promotion, she had to do the work with excellence to earn it. So she performed her best with all of her assignments. Gina was promoted to a full-time day-shift cardiac stress position a year and a half after being hired. The position required certification in two areas. She studied for the credentialing examinations and passed each on the first attempt. She worked in cardiac stress testing for five years. She was successful and knowledgeable in her role, but it didn't come without the price of hard work, commitment, and dedication. Her pay increased substantially with each promotion she acquired.

Gina understood the value of knowledge early in her career. She was trained primarily by doctors, directors, and managers while working as a stress technologist. She observed and learned the language and processes of management along with the protocols and treatment executed by physicians. She realized she was strategically positioned around top talent who could groom her for leadership. Therefore, she seized the moments and learned everything she could from them. They shared a wealth of knowledge with her.

She decided to go back to school full-time to become a cardiac sonographer. Cardiac sonography was the highest position in noninvasive cardiology next to management. Hospitals listed the position as key because it was difficult to find credentialed individuals to fill the position, and the salary was good. Returning to school was a bittersweet challenge for Gina. She had to manage being a full-time employee, full-time student, and a single mother all at once. Through sacrifice and commitment, she persevered and obtained her credentials as a registered diagnostic cardiac sonographer. The position increased her pay by $34,000 over the span of three years.

In her new role, she did cardiac imaging and procedures and trained new hires, employees, and new cardiology fellows. Management delegated several duties and roles to her, and she took them on without complaint. This led her to further develop a mastery of skills and possess a higher level of competency in the areas of supervision, testing, technology, protocols, and equipment functionality. Her knowledge and expertise made it hard for others to deny her as the go-to person of the department. Her talent was recognized by management, who was impressed by her performance. They admired how Gina diplomatically interacted with employees, patients, and other departmental staff. Since she was credentialed in various areas and close to obtaining a Bachelor of Science in Business Administration, the chief of cardiology, director of cardiology, and the vice president of the hospital collaboratively agreed to make Gina an offer to manage three areas within the cardiology division. The position placed her over EKG, EEG, and cardiac sonography imaging. She reported to the director and chief physician of cardiology. It was her first position in leadership. Gina was moved from the back technical area to her very own office. She learned the business end of the hospital and what made it profitable. In her new, prestigious role, she learned additional policies and procedures from management's prospective, including human resources management, utilization review, and risk management. She stayed in the position for three years until she was informed that the hospital would soon close.

Gina applied at a state-of-the-art level-one trauma hospital, one of the best in the state. With her years of experience in cardiology, she was considered a senior sonographer in the field. The hospital hired her to work in their accredited noninvasive lab. There, she learned industry standards, best practices, and how to effectively service patients with advanced cardiac illnesses and diseases. While working there, Gina completed a Master of Science in Management and Leadership and became eligible for another promotion in leadership. The district director had promised to promote Gina but failed to do so. However, there was something better waiting for her despite the disappointment. She later learned of an online posting for a director of the cardiovascular technology program at a nearby college. She submitted an online résumé and applied for the job. The president of the college took interest in her résumé and called Gina for an interview with himself and the vice president of academic affairs.

After careful consideration of her academic and technical skills, credentials, and work history, Gina was offered the position, which came with a competitive wage, bonuses, and an attractive benefit package. She became the director of several cohorts of students, clinical, and adjunct instructors. She worked diligently to get the program accredited, and after three years of hard work and dedication, the program was granted accreditation, the only associated degree program accredited in the state of Michigan.

Gina went from the bottom to the top of her profession over time. She received many accolades during her career, and she obtained several student retention awards and conducted educational presentations at the local hospitals and schools. She is acknowledged as a leader in her field and was accepted as a fellow with the American Society of Echocardiography (FASE). Gina never stopped developing and educating others. Today, she works periodically in the field of cardiology and at a local college. She teaches various allied health courses to those who will later become medical professionals in our communities.

Gina's definition of success:

"Success to me is defined as being where you want to be in life and doing what you love to do. It's discovering and unveiling your call in life. It's being aware of who you are and what you were born to do. It begins with the perspective of knowing where you are and where you want to go. It's recognizing and developing your talents and honing your

skills. Success is monitoring your progress and considering the sacrifices you must make. It's reaching your potential in the various areas where you are inspired the most. Success is measured in both short-term increments and long-term planning and execution. Potential is met when goals are accomplished. When goals are accomplished, that equals success! Success is the ultimate feeling of self-fulfillment, both socially and professionally. In all actuality, it's loving who you are and what you've become!"

AUTHOR'S COMMENTARY:

What a wonderful career and testimony. Gina's story proves that nothing is too hard for you to achieve as long as you are willing to put in the hard work and sacrifice. Gina possessed not only the hard skills of her field but also the soft skills. You can't be truly successful without both. She also possessed business character. Gina had the whole package! She was known for her diplomacy with her staff, patients, and coworkers. Her testimony is an example of her gift making room for her and bringing her before great men such as the chief and director of cardiology and the vice president of the hospital. Gina realized that in order to be successful, she had to unveil her professional calling. Now, she is a known expert in the field of cardiology.

Gregory, *entrepreneur*

Gregory dreamed of earning a degree or certification in his field as an environmental specialist. At the time, the profession wasn't popular, so finding a school that offered a licensing certification would be difficult. In fact, there were no local schools offering the program, but God gave Gregory the insight to research schools out of state. His research went well, and he found a highly qualified training institute in another state. Gregory was passionate about his training credentials because of the harmful effects lead poisoning had on the children in the Detroit metropolitan area. Detroit, Hamtramck, and Highland Park had a large number of older homes, many of which were considered historical by the state of Michigan. But these homes were known to have high concentrations of lead-based paint. The demand for lead-based paint inspections for these homes was great. Gregory decided to present information about the training to his employer, but the company didn't want to pay for the training, even though the certification would have been beneficial to both his company and him. But Gregory was so determined that he informed his employer he would pay for it himself and use his vacation days to attend the training.

Once he acquired the license, his company couldn't use it since he had paid for it himself. He was only the third person in Michigan to have the license. During that time, the housing market crashed across the nation. People were losing their homes left and right because of foreclosures, and most of the homes were falling into the banks' hands. The banks had a surplus of houses to sell, and each one of the homes had to be inspected for lead-based paint before being resold or placed on the market. Gregory received a call from his pastor, Dr. Stacks, and she asked him, "How is your job going?"

He explained that he was frustrated with the job because they had refused to pay or reimburse him for training that would've been beneficial to them both. He was dissatisfied with other things at the job as well. After listening to all of Gregory's concerns, his pastor immediately began praying. During the prayer, God gave the pastor a revelation about Gregory's situation that would change his whole outlook on life and his career. She asked the Lord to bless him with his own business. Gregory immediately stopped her and told her he had already started an environmental company two years prior and even had a name for it, but he hadn't done anything with the business. Dr. Stacks asked him why not. And that was a good question. Gregory already had everything set up for the business. They began to pray that his business would take off.

Three days later, Gregory received a phone call from a potential client, looking for Michigan lead-based paint inspectors. Gregory was wary of the client, so he asked the client to send him detailed information about the job. The client sent all the information, and he kept calling, asking when he could start working. Frustrated, the client finally asked, "What's the hold up? I'm going to send you a number of houses. Can you perform the lead inspections and get the reports back to me?"

Gregory was still working at his current job. He was unhappy and only inspecting four houses a day. The client wanted him to increase his inspections to eight per day. In fact, Gregory could inspect up to fifteen if he had his own machine and staff. When the client called again, Gregory told him he could inspect at least ten houses per day and provide the report that same day, but the price of the machine he needed to do the job was $20,000. He didn't have the money, and his wife had just given birth to their first child after complications. He was skeptical about quitting his job and pursuing his own business full-time. He needed the health insurance for his wife and child, but he could see how God was working on his behalf.

When the client found out Gregory didn't have his own machine, he asked him to give him three days to see what he could do for him. That following Sunday, Gregory talked to Dr. Stacks regarding the opportunity, and she was astonished. He explained to her that the issue was that he didn't have the proper equipment to do the job or the money to get it. But Dr. Stacks had prayed that the business would be more prosperous than anything Gregory had ever seen. The next morning, Gregory received a phone call from the client. "If you can inspect eight houses a day, we will supply you with a machine and pay you weekly for every house you complete." The offer was unheard of. Gregory had never expected someone to pay him within a week per house and supply him with the equipment. What happened next was just God. The client agreed to pay him $200 per house and they would work out a payment plan for the machine.

Now that Gregory was a contractor for the client, he immediately quit his job because he knew that God had given him the business and it would be blessed. Within the next week, Gregory completed twelve houses a day for $2,400. He was blessed to get his own equipment and staff, and the business prospered. He went to church with tithes in his hand, and Dr. Stacks simply said she had never seen God be so close to their prayers.

Ten years later, Gregory said, "You know, we pray these prayers, and we ask God for all these things, but we never stretch out on Him. I look back now, ten years later, and realize He has kept me and blessed me all this time. God is waiting for us to have enough faith to believe Him. It was a faith walk for me to quit my job after my wife had just had our baby. I had to trust Him for everything: insurance, rent, food. But He proved Himself to me. If we would just trust Him and let Him be God, the outcome will be great!"

Gregory's definition of success:
"Having a spiritual and natural inheritance from God, which will enable you to leave an effective legacy after you're gone. Believing that my prayers and the sowing of seeds will empower the next generation to come."

AUTHOR'S COMMENTARY:

Gregory's testimony is beautiful! He had a passion for his career, and he pursued it. When his job refused to fund his education for his license, he didn't let that stop him. When he received his license for environmental inspection, the clients came looking for him. This was his calling and his gift made room for him in the business world. But Gregory still had to take a leap of faith at a trying time in his life. Dr. Stacks, his pastor and mentor, gave him the insight and confidence to do it. She believed in him and encouraged him to pursue his dream. Sometimes, we need a mentor to encourage, support, and empower us. When he took the leap of faith, the blessings overflowed, and now, Gregory is a successful entrepreneur. He will empower the next generation to come with his testimony.

Jennifer, *medical doctor*

Jennifer always had a love for learning. She'd enjoyed it ever since she was a little girl. Nothing was too hard to tackle. Medicine was always the field for her because it was exciting, interesting, and challenging. New things were always happening or being discovered in the medical field, and Jennifer wanted to be a part of it. She admired doctors because they worked so hard, and she believed caring for the lives of others was a great responsibility. She wanted that responsibility as well, and she wanted to commit her life to a profession that was meaningful and full of purpose.

A tremendous amount of hard work was required for Jennifer to reach her goals. She had to complete four years of undergraduate school, four years of medical school, and three years of residency—a total of eleven years of intense studying, training, and learning. It was time consuming and required an enormous amount of sacrifice. Many days were overwhelming and exhausting. Jennifer had to take numerous tests and board exams, and the road was not always easy.

While in medical school, Jennifer married a wonderful man and had two beautiful children. Being a wife and mother added another level of responsibility to Jennifer's already hectic life. She took some time away from school to focus on her family. But after much thought and prayer, she decided this path was her calling, and she wanted to complete the process. Jennifer believed God was with her every step of the way. She was blessed to be surrounded by people who loved and supported her and prayed for her throughout the process. Jennifer's husband also supported her endlessly and never made her choose between her career path and her family.

One of the most influential people in Jennifer's life was her grandmother, Dr. Stacks, who was also her pastor. Her wisdom and guidance gave Jennifer clarity during her toughest times. Jennifer appreciated her grandmother's love, support, and prayers. She always pushed her to reach her full potential, not only naturally but spiritually. When Jennifer took her first board exam in medical school, it was difficult, and she didn't pass. She was feeling overwhelmed and wasn't sure if she should continue with medical school. Shortly after deciding to take time away from school, she attended a service in Baltimore, MD, where Dr. Stacks was speaking. During the service, she prayed for Jennifer, and it was life changing. The prayer confirmed the things she had been feeling, and God gave her a renewed strength to finish her journey.

Dr. Stacks told her, "It's time for you to finish." From then on, Jennifer didn't have any hindrances regarding school, classes, exams, rotations, or personal issues that would delay her progress. Jennifer was grateful that Dr. Stacks' instruction and teachings allowed her to build a closer relationship with God.

In 2018, Jennifer completed her family medicine residency and became board certified. She is currently working as the lead bariatrician in the bariatric surgery division, providing excellent care for patients looking to lead healthier lives. To God be all the glory!

Jennifer's definition of success:

"Success is walking in the purpose and plan God has for your life."

AUTHOR'S COMMENTARY:

Jennifer's dream of becoming a doctor came with hard work and sacrifice. But, more importantly, when the circumstances of life got in her way, she persevered. Jennifer stayed true to her calling. When she hit rough times, she simply took time off. Occasionally, you may have to step away to reflect, refocus, and get rejuvenated in your calling.

Jennifer's gift made room for her and brought her before great men. Her pastor was the great person in Jennifer's life who supported her, prayed for her, and gave her the wisdom and guidance she needed. You may not be able to accomplish your professional calling on your own. You'll need others who believe in you and see your potential. The workings of the Lord were mighty in Jennifer's life. Now, she's walking in her purpose and her professional calling!

Final Comments:

All these businessmen and women had faith in their professional callings and purpose. The career testimonies are powerful and encouraging. If they can do it, so can you. Each story was unique, but they all started out the same—with a dream. I believe no dream is too hard to accomplish. What about you?

CHAPTER 8
SUCCESS IS WAITING ON YOU!

Success! What we've all been waiting for and dreaming of. But you're not waiting on success; success is waiting on you. What's between you and success? Is it your daily plans, or is it procrastination because you are not following through? It should be the implementation of your plans and goals, pursuing them daily, which will lead you to success. Speed up and do what you have to do. Everything is inside you already. You must take the strategic steps to ignite that desire and follow through. You can have a desire inside you, but if you don't take action and embrace your dreams, it will never come to fruition. Success is pursuing your dreams and accomplishing your goals. Don't keep success waiting too long!

What's Your Definition of Success?

Success means favorable outcomes, results, and one that succeeds. All the attributes that we have discussed. What's your definition of success? All the professionals who gave testimonials also provided their definitions of success. What's yours? It can mean different things to different people. Is it the big house on the hill with an attached three-car garage for your luxury cars? Is it owning a business and grossing millions of dollars annually? Or does it mean obtaining that great job in the corporate world or having your own business and being your own boss? Maybe it's having a loving husband or wife and a wonderful family to go home to every day. Perhaps it's good health for you and your family. What about helping others and giving of yourself? Is it having peace with our Lord? None of the professionals mentioned big houses or millions of dollars. Their definitions were humble and sound, yet they're all successful. Let's be clear—salary and wages are important. There's nothing wrong with earning a lucrative income. You want to be able to take care of your family, home, education for your children, and retirement for you and your spouse. Savings are crucial and wise. To invest into savings accounts, IRA's, and annuity accounts, it takes a good income. Financial independence is one of the goals we're aiming for in our professional calling. Some of us will make millions and others will not, but having a career in which you excel and you love doing every day is a rewarding experience.

So what's your definition of success? It could be everything I've stated or maybe I didn't quite touch on your personal definition. Think about it and write it down in your journal or on your notepad, and go back from time to time to reflect about your journey to success. It will solidify the successes you're working toward.

Let's talk about what it's going to take to accomplish your business successes.

Go Above and Beyond

You must go above and beyond the call of duty to be successful. You have a duty to yourself and your dreams. Your duty right now is to prepare for your future by pursuing your professional calling and traveling the path you have laid out for yourself through the planning and implementation process outlined in Chapter Two. You must take action. You must study hard, work hard, and pray hard. There are success stories about people who started out homeless, sleeping in their cars or being down and out with nothing in their pockets. Those individuals didn't give up because of their circumstances. They were committed to working hard to obtain their goals until they became successful despite their situations. Many of us have a place to stay and money in our pockets, so we're starting out with more. Maybe not, but the amazing part of this is that those individuals had a burning desire and did more with less. What are you doing with what you have?

Nothing about success is easy. Going above and beyond means that sometimes you'll have to be the first one at the job and the last one to leave. It means going that extra mile in all your business dealings to ensure the customer is satisfied and will return. It's making your mark in your profession to identify yourself as the best in your career. Going above and beyond means not being a victim of your circumstances. Sometimes, we allow our circumstances to stop us from achieving what is rightfully ours. Don't let your past, your circumstances, or other people stop you from working hard to obtain your dreams. Go above it and go beyond it. Keep moving toward the goals, plans, and dreams that will lead you to your success.

Mindset

Your mindset is important to your success. Focus on positive thoughts that give you confidence. Don't allow negative thoughts to overtake your mind. The scripture says, "For as he thinketh in his heart, so is he." (Proverbs 23:7 KJV). Think about being that successful businessman or woman, or think about being the best at whatever your career goal is. Think positive. Don't think low. Low thoughts will bring you down. Our thoughts determine our outcomes. Concentrate on having a positive attitude and disposition about achieving goals. It affects your mood and energy. Concentrate on achieving and receiving your blessing. Don't let mistakes or disappointments detour your mindset. Learn from mistakes and accept disappointments by focusing on what you could have done better. Use them as learning tools and steppingstones.

When I began my HR career, I had to tell myself repeatedly that I wasn't going back to my old job. The new position seemed so hard and I was overwhelmed. At times, I couldn't see the light at the end of the tunnel. But I didn't allow my mind to take me down. That's were faith comes in, believing that you can accomplish something that seems unattainable. I had to fight with faith and determination. I kept telling myself that I could do it, and I did. I believed in myself, and I believed I could achieve my goals. You must believe in yourself, your talents, and your abilities. A positive mindset thrives on persistence no matter what happens. And you must have this mindset daily. Not only will your actions be positive, but your outcomes will, too.

A Desire to Succeed

You must have a desire to succeed to be successful. Your desire has to be so strong that it propels you into the course of action you must take to reach your goals. The definition of success mentions the word "succeed" twice because succeeding is a big part of your success. To succeed is to attain a desired goal or objective. It means to achieve something. As you plan and achieve your goals, you are succeeding in your endeavors to be successful. The road map to succeed has been outlined for you in the previous chapters. Follow the road map to your success. Each day that you succeed on your career path is a positive step toward your success. Make each day count, even if the day didn't turn out well for you. Use it as a learning experience. Succeeding is learning, growing, achieving, and striving to reach every goal. When you succeed, you bring forth the reward of your labor.

Overcome Your Fears

We all experience fear. Maybe you're about to speak in front of a large audience; you don't know them, and they don't know you. Seconds before going to the podium, you get butterflies in your stomach. You feel the fear and anxiety, but despite all obstacles, you step right up to the podium and deliver your speech. Mission accomplished! It's natural to feel fear in certain situations, but you must always step forward and deliver. This is how we conquer our fears; we keep stepping forward and deliver on the plans we have set in place. Don't step back; step forward and overcome the fear. Doing so builds your confidence and your faith that you can conquer every obstacle on your path.

Many of us fear failure, but failure isn't always a bad thing. You can learn a great deal from failures. And sometimes failing is necessary for us to find our way.

President Franklin Roosevelt failed the bar association exam. Former First Lady Michelle Obama also failed the bar exam, but they both went on to pass on their second attempt and had successful careers that took them all the way to the white house! I'm sure President Roosevelt and Michelle Obama learned something from their failures. Allow your failures to make you wiser. When you fail at something, don't beat yourself up. Be gentle with yourself but vigilant, with the confidence that you know you're going to bounce back even better than before. That's how successful people respond to failure. You can overcome all your fears on this journey and walk the path of success.

CHAPTER 9

THE SECRETS OF YOUR PROFESSIONAL CALLING

The secret of your professional calling is branching out into other areas because of the expertise you've acquired in your calling.

Growing and Developing in Your Career

Growth is important in your career choice. You can't just stay stagnate. Growing and developing takes you to the expert level of your career. Embrace growth and development by doing the following:

- Find a mentor or master trainer in your field who is willing to take you under their wing and teach you. This type of relationship is valuable because you will get the benefits of one-on-one training, which is much better than a classroom or group setting. I was blessed to have a manager who was an excellent trainer. I obtained a wealth of knowledge from my manager and gained a valuable friend and mentor. Daralynn didn't have any experience recruiting engineers, but her team leader, who was a skilled engineer recruiter, saw Daralynn's potential and trained her step-by-step through the recruiting and hiring process for engineers. Because of the training and guidance Daralynn received from her team leader, she became proficient in her field, and her team leader became her mentor and friend.

- Continue to learn. Embrace lifelong learning through the pursuit of maintaining current industry standards and practices of your profession. Join organizations or professional subscriptions. Also, attend professional conferences and keep all licenses and certifications required by your profession current. This self-directed learning adds to your skills and knowledge. Always have a hunger for knowledge. Take advantage of all the workshops, courses, seminars, and training your employer offers. Network with professional groups and colleagues outside of the workplace. If your job updates their business systems or introduces new technology, be the first to be trained. Don't draw back. Learning advances you, so you'll be ready for the next level in your career.

- Embrace change. Always be open for new experiences and change in the workplace. Be flexible and have a positive attitude. Sometimes, we shy away from change and new trends, but, often, change is good. Don't be stuck in one place and one way of doing things. Embrace change and flow with it. It's always an imminent factor in the workplace. Change is constant. It allows you to learn how to do things differently, but you must have an open mind.

- There will be times when a new manager or CEO will come aboard, and with the change of leadership will come new expectations and requirements. Don't let it overwhelm you. Be a team player and confident that you can learn and master all new processes and assignments. Doing so will prepare you for anything that comes your way, allowing you to be a valuable employee.

- Going outside of your comfort zone will stimulate growth because you will learn different things. While I was working in human resources, I serviced as many as thirty departments. I learned so much from each department because I was willing to go outside of my comfort zone. Some of my colleagues serviced only one department and didn't want to be assigned anywhere else. You limit your knowledge and growth when you stay in one place, but when you go outside of your comfort zone, you gain knowledge and build relationships. Don't move haphazardly but with wisdom, purpose, and focus, knowing that you're going in the right direction according to the plan you have for your career.

Be Creative

Being creative is a part of success. Whatever your career or business calling is, you should become the best at it. When you know all the ins and outs of a career or business, you can start letting your creativity flow and make innovative improvements to the service you're providing. You may have ideas to reassess customers' needs, review the vision and mission of the company, or optimize quality assurance, which will benefit all. If you have an idea or project, follow through on it. Collaborate with others. Get a team and work on the creative project. Be open to feedback and constructive criticism to further fuel the idea.

If you feel like you're not naturally creative, do something that stimulates your creative side. Take a walk on a nature trail. I love walking and thinking. It's so relaxing.

Sometimes, just taking a walk alone can trigger your thought process and creativity. Try listening to music, going to the gym, doing yoga, or writing. Your surroundings are important also. Your environment must be conducive to creativity. Find your creative place. Successful people are creative people.

Have a Global Business Outlook

A global business outlook is a necessity in our workforce today. Your goal should be to market your business and services or your company to the world. Whether you're an entrepreneur or employed by a large firm, global thinking is an asset for your career. Many of the large corporations in the United States have corporate offices in other countries. Being sensitive to the cultures and lifestyles of other countries is key. Social media platforms like Facebook, Twitter, LinkedIn, Instagram, and YouTube connect you to the global business world, allowing companies to market their goods and services all over the world.

Become an Expert in Your Career

After you've been in your field for some time, the training and experience you have acquired over the years will qualify you as an expert. Gina, the director of cardiovascular technology and Deborah, the dean of health careers and sciences, went on to become experts in their fields. Becoming an expert isn't easy. It takes time. You'll go through many transitions and positions in your career prior to reaching the expert level. For some professionals, the next step will be an upper level management position, which will take you into another phase of your professional calling. Sometimes, we must be pushed to apply for that type of promotion because we're in our comfort zone. In order to optimize your career potential, you must take every step. My former mentor and manager encouraged me to apply for my first management position. I was a little skeptical, but it was the right move. Management was a whole new ballgame for me, and it stimulated by learning and growth all over again. It led me to where I am now: a writer, speaker, and HR advisor. Sometimes, one career leads to another.

There are other ways to establish yourself as an expert:
- Become a mentor
- Write a blog
- Be a speaker
- Write a book
- Be a coach
- Become a consultant
- Host a webinar
- Be a trainer

- Be a teacher
- Become a subject matter expert
- Host a lunch and learn session
- Produce an email newsletter

My choice was, of course, writing a book. Your professional calling can lead you into other directions after becoming an expert in your field.

Can You Have More Than One Professional Calling?

Absolutely! You can have more than one professional calling. Daralynn is a successful author and HR recruiter. I have a friend who is a systems analyst for a major university and on evenings and weekends, she's an event planner. She loves it! Both are pursing two careers at the same time. You may have a well-paying profession like a nurse but during the evenings and weekends, you may be a makeup artist, website developer, or social media manager. You can be a full-timer with a business or job on the side. The other job may be a hobby of yours or another career. Many people juggle more than one job and pursue more than one passion. It can open huge doors of opportunities.

Multiple Careers

Millennials and Generation Y are gravitating toward slasher careers. "Slasher" refers to the slash mark to indicate multiple professions. For example: biologist/songwriter/blogger or teacher/consultant/DJ/singer. Many are stepping outside of the traditional guidelines for careers. They may have dual, triple, or quadruple careers. Most slashers are entrepreneurs, and this group is growing fast. They have a diverse set of skills that they utilize in all their career choices. One of my family members is a slasher in her own right. She's an accountant/model/promoter/student. Slashers don't fit into the traditional career mindset. They step out of the box. The sky is the limit. If you can dream it, you can be it. I love this group because they are living their lives to the fullest, with résumés that boast many diverse skillsets.

THE BENEFITS

There are benefits to having more than one career.

1. Personal growth: You are growing in other areas, which opens a wealth of opportunities.

2. Increased income: Everyone can use an additional income stream in our economy today. The funds can be used to increase your 401K or for special projects around your home. Having extra money saved for family vacations and travel is great as well.

3. Doing what you enjoy and having a more fulfilling life: Having another interest that you enjoy and earning extra money from doing what you enjoy is a win-win situation. Also, doing something different outside of your regular career helps to eliminate boredom and gives your life a little variety.

4. It stimulates you: Having two jobs will keep you on your toes.

THE DOWNSIDE

1. Balance: Don't work too many hours. Overextending yourself can lead to burnout. Know your limits. You want to perform your best each day, so you must get enough rest and eat healthy. Your primary career is your main focus because it's the bread-and-butter career on which you balance your budget.

2. Not for everyone: Some professionals only want one career, and that's fine for them. I focused on just one career at a time. But that was me. Everyone is different. At the end of the day, you must do what you feel is your niche. Whether it's one career or multiple careers, you must decide what's best for your life.

RULES TO FOLLOW WITH TWO OR MORE CAREERS

Ensure that you follow all your employer's policies and procedures. Some employers require that you inform them of any self-employment or outside employment. All this information should have been provided to you during the onboarding process. The company wants to ensure there is no conflict of interest. They may ask you the hours and times you work for your other job, the name of the other company, and the services you provide to determine whether you're double dipping or daylighting, which means working two jobs during the same work hours, a practice that is considered unethical. That type of behavior can lead to termination. When you follow the ethical rules of having multiple careers, you'll reap the benefits.

The secrets of your professional calling are broad and give you plenty of opportunities for advancement. That's what you want to do, advance in your career and achieve the highest level in your professional calling.

CHAPTER 10
THE TAKEAWAY

The career and professional development resources I've provided are intended to prepare you to succeed in the business world. You don't have to stay in a stagnated job. You can climb out of the barrel. I hope my testimony and the testimonies of others inspired you to step out and achieve your goals. You can move into the career of your dreams and your professional calling. No matter what your career of choice is, you are a part of the global workforce, which places you in the business world. If you're part of such a huge global industry, why not succeed? Succeeding leads to success. To be successful, you must succeed in your plans, goals, education, and training. I have provided you with effective tools and resources. Utilize and embrace them. My desire for you is to achieve a rewarding and fulfilling career.

It's time to reach for the sky and soar to your dream career. Implement your plan today!

REFERENCES

1. O'Donnell, J.T. (2018, January 22). I Spent 15 Years Studying Why People Hate Their Jobs. This Is the Top Reason. Retrieved from https://www.inc.com/jt-odonnell/how-this-1-question-can-make-you-choose-wrong-career.html

2. SMART Goals. (2019). Retrieved from Mindtools.com/pages/article/smart-goals.htm

3. More Than Half of Employers Have Found Content on Social Media That Caused Them NOT to Hire a Candidate, According to Recent CareerBuilder Survey. (2019). Retrieved from http://press.careerbuilder.com/2018-08-09-More-Than-Half-of-Employers-Have-Found-Content-on-Social-Media-That-Caused-Them-NOT-to-Hire-a-Candidate-According-to-Recent-CareerBuilder-Survey

4. Wikipedia, the free Encyclopedia. (2019). Soft Skills. Retrieved from https://en.wikipedia.org/wiki/Soft_skills

www.ingramcontent.com/pod-product-compliance
Lightning Source LLC
Chambersburg PA
CBHW021408290426
44108CB00010B/444